The Power of Teacher Rounds

A Guide for Facilitators, Principals, & Department Chairs

Vivian Troen

Katherine C. Boles

With Jacob Pinnolis and Aviva Scheur

Foreword by Richard F. Elmore

CORWIN
A SAGE Company

learningforward

CORWIN
A SAGE Company

FOR INFORMATION:

Corwin
A SAGE Company
2455 Teller Road
Thousand Oaks, California 91320
(800) 233-9936
www.corwin.com

SAGE Publications Ltd.
1 Oliver's Yard
55 City Road
London EC1Y 1SP
United Kingdom

SAGE Publications India Pvt. Ltd.
B 1/I 1 Mohan Cooperative Industrial Area
Mathura Road, New Delhi 110 044
India

SAGE Publications Asia-Pacific Pte. Ltd.
3 Church Street
#10-04 Samsung Hub
Singapore 049483

Acquisitions Editor: Dan Alpert
Associate Editor: Kimberly Greenberg
Editorial Assistant: Cesar Reyes
Production Editor: Libby Larson
Copy Editor: Megan Granger
Typesetter: C&M Digitals (P) Ltd.
Proofreader: Rae-Ann Goodwin
Indexer: Michael Ferreira
Cover Designer: Shawn Girsberger
Marketing Manager: Lisa Lysne

Copyright © 2014 by Corwin

Printed in the United States of America.

Library of Congress Cataloging-in-Publication Data

Troen, Vivian, 1940–
The power of teacher rounds: a guide for facilitators, principals, & department chairs / Vivian Troen, Katherine C. Boles ; with Jacob Pinnolis and Aviva Scheur.

pages cm
Includes bibliographical references and index.

ISBN 978-1-4833-4995-4 (pbk.)
ISBN 978-1-4833-4996-1 (web pdf)

1. Observation (Educational method)—United States. 2. Teachers—In-service training—United States. I. Boles, Katherine. II. Title.

LB1027.28.T76 2014
370.71'1—dc23   2014006001

This book is printed on acid-free paper.

FSC
www.fsc.org

MIX
Paper from
responsible sources
FSC® C014174

14 15 16 17 18 10 9 8 7 6 5 4 3 2 1

The Power of Teacher Rounds

Today's teachers have at their disposal tremendous amounts of information about teaching but there are few practical guides on how to use that information to improve their practice. Troen and Boles help to remedy this with The Power of Teacher Rounds. *Complete with actual case studies and infused with theoretical underpinnings, this book should be in the hands (not just on the shelf) of every teacher, principal and district leader committed to improving student learning through improvements in teacher practice.*

—Irvin Scott
Deputy Director of Education
Bill & Melinda Gates Foundation

Troen and Boles are quintessential practitioners who want all teachers to have access to the very best methods for improving their practice. In The Power of Teacher Rounds, *these practitioner/authors have made the process of collaborative improvement available for everyone. I will use this book immediately!*

—Patricia Wasley
CEO, Teaching Channel

As educators implement the CCSS, collaboration is essential. With The Power of Teacher Rounds, *Troen and Boles have made a major contribution in providing educators—who often work in isolation—with exemplars of modeling and learning from one another.*

—Katherine Bassett
CEO, National Network of State Teachers of the Year
2000 New Jersey State Teacher of the Year

At the Eliot K–8 Innovation School, we have been thrilled to embrace and fully implement the practices so amazingly presented in this book and are excited about the outcomes. Vivian and Kitty have captured the strategies that have allowed the teachers at the Eliot to implement Teacher Rounds in small teacher teams, and our professional learning community is thriving as a result. We owe them our thanks for continuing to believe in the work of teachers by writing a book that provides teacher teams with a straightforward way to share and grow a practice that will strengthen the instructional core.

—Traci Walker Griffith, Principal
Eliot K–8 Innovation School, Boston (MA)

Troen and Boles provide a true alternative to the external models of school reform, empowering the people working in schools to create change. With The Power of Teacher Rounds, *they show how teachers can improve student learning by building capacity within themselves and throughout the school. Troen and Boles show the way to replace a long-standing culture of teacher isolation with a new culture of critical colleagueship, creating a more powerful framework for teachers' professional learning.*

—David Goldfarb
Principal
Fairfax (VA) High School

One of the things we should do more of in education is to deeply engage teachers in the design of solutions for improving their practice and advancing the learning of their students. The Power of Teacher Rounds *details just such an opportunity: engaging teachers in collaborative, growth-producing professional learning anchored in their explicit needs and context. Teacher Rounds is not a simple exercise or a magic bullet. Rather it requires that teachers deeply immerse themselves in observations, discussions and feedback on successful practice and commit themselves to continuous improvement. In a world of ineffective, one-size-fits-all professional development, this how-to guide illustrates how powerful and empowering for teachers that can be.*

—Vicki Phillips
Director of Education—College Ready
Bill & Melinda Gates Foundation

The Power of Teacher Rounds *gives us a powerful step forward in finding the "holy grail of education"—the answer to how do we change a teacher's practice. Troen and Boles present a step-by-step process that serves as a guide for those who seek systemic improvement. I recommend this book as a must read for all educators.*

—Shimon Waronker
Founder, The New American Academies
New York City P.S. 770, P.S. 274, TNAA Charter School

The authors of The Power of Teacher Rounds *have created a roadmap to supercharge professional learning communities. They have written a practical "how-to" guide with real-life case studies and guiding tools for teacher leaders, principals, and district administrators who are looking to develop a model of collaborative observation. As a superintendent who has led district-wide instructional rounds with administrators, I know that this book will be an invaluable resource for expanding our work to teachers at the classroom level.*

—Kenneth N. Salim
Superintendent, Weymouth Public Schools
Past President, Learning Forward

As increasing emphasis is being placed on teachers collaborating with one another to improve student learning, there are few really practical guides for doing so. Now Troen and Boles, pioneers of teacher leadership from the classroom, bring us a groundbreaking book on teacher rounds—a strategy they powerfully demonstrate can be a pathway toward meeting the Common Core State Standards.

—Barnett Berry
CEO, Center for Teaching Quality

Highly informative, full of processes, protocols, and cases, The Power of Teacher Rounds *is a knowing and practical guide for those who want to leverage teacher rounds for authentic teacher learning and the continuous development of practice. Facilitators will greatly appreciate it as a detailed manual on how to implement teacher rounds so as to have real and lasting impact.*

—Thomas Del Prete
Director, Adam Institute for Urban Teaching and School Practice
Author of *Teacher Rounds: A Guide to Collaborative Learning in and From Practice*

This is truly a great book and one that I think will inspire teachers to take ownership of their learning, use each other as professional development resources and de-privatize their practice in an effort to change teaching practice and improve student learning. The Power of Teacher Rounds *values the intellectual work of teachers and demonstrates how they can be leaders of their own ongoing learning through teacher collaboration and professional learning communities.*

—Shakera Walker
Senior Manager, Teacher Leadership
Boston Public Schools

Vivian Troen and Kitty Boles and are among this country's leading thinkers on improving teacher quality and classroom practice. In their previous book, Who's Teaching Your Children?, *they accurately assessed the need to improve teacher preparation and change the professional culture within America's schools. Their book* The Power of Teacher Teams *provided a groundbreaking guide for teachers and school leaders to navigate through the obstacles of collaborative teams. Now,* The Power of Teacher Rounds *expands on that important work by outlining a process of analysis and discourse through which teachers can increase their instructional capacity. This book offers a practical guide for teachers, coaches, administrators, and anyone else who is interested in leading truly meaningful professional development at the school level.*

—Joel D. Boyd
Superintendent
Santa Fe (NM) Public Schools

Troen and Boles have crafted a completely teacher-driven process that inspires improved teaching across grade levels, issuing a call to Rounds that goes beyond studying data and student work. They challenge teachers to identify a compelling problem of practice, share it across a grade level team and honor the insights it generates in their teaching practice. The Power of Teacher Rounds *offers a practical way to balance instructional capacity and accountability, which is what most schools are trying to do.*

—MAK Mitchell
Former Executive Director of School Governance
New York City Department of Education

In The Power of Teacher Rounds, *Vivian Troen and Kitty Boles serve as expert guides in using the innovative and groundbreaking collaborative practice of teacher rounds. Drawing on these experienced teachers' deep expertise, this book is a must-have for anyone interested in achieving excellence in classroom teaching. Vivian and Kitty articulate an exciting and important vision for the teaching profession, employing a process that can be implemented within a school's existing budget and calendar. This book, with its clarifying case studies and informative videos, should be an integral part of teacher training and leadership development initiatives in public, charter, independent, and faith-based schools.*

—Mary Grassa O'Neill
Former Secretary for Education/Superintendent, Archdiocese of Boston
Senior Lecturer, Harvard Graduate School of Education

Contents

All materials and resources related to *The Power of Teacher Rounds*—including reproducible figures, tables, handouts, worksheets, and appendices—can be found at http://www.corwin.com/powerofteacherrounds

Figures

All materials and resources related to *The Power of Teacher Rounds*—including reproducible figures, tables, handouts, worksheets, and appendices—can be found at http://www.corwin .com/powerofteacherrounds

Videos

All materials and resources related to *The Power of Teacher Rounds*—including reproducible figures, tables, handouts, worksheets, and appendices—can be found at http://www.corwin.com/powerofteacherrounds

Foreword

Richard F. Elmore

Gregory R. Anrig Professor of Educational Leadership, Harvard Graduate School of Education

In the fifteen years or so since I began the practice of what we now call "instructional rounds," I have observed upwards of 2,000 classrooms in roughly 500 schools across 30 or 40 school systems in five countries. In this period of time, I have seen the complexity of teachers' work change dramatically with the introduction of new, more cognitively challenging curricula; the increasing salience of external student assessments; the now near-universal use of teacher teams; and the introduction of various forms of teacher evaluation and support. The work of teaching has always been complex and demanding for those who take student learning seriously. The focus and intensity of the current period of "school reform" have made it more so. But what have we done to increase the capability of teachers to manage this complexity? It sometimes seems to me that everyone has at least one big idea about something teachers should be doing, but very few have any idea about how to make all these big ideas cohere into a job that mere mortals can do and still have a little time left over to walk the dog, shop for groceries, hug a child, and take out the trash.

We are now at or near the limit of how much more we can ask teachers to do without changing, in some fundamental way, how we define the work of teaching. The most basic understanding of the neuroscience of learning would lead us to question the way we organize the practice of teaching and learning. Think, for example, about the learning demands for teachers and students embodied in the Common Core State Standards—the latest bright, shiny object in the firmament of school reform. A cursory look at the standards will tell anyone who has any grasp of what American classrooms currently look like that both teachers and students are being asked to engage in practices of teaching and learning for which they have little or no preparation. We are asking teachers to engage students in types of learning that *they, the teachers, have never experienced themselves.* We talk about "implementing" the Common Core State Standards as if it were the equivalent of installing a catalytic converter in an automobile or updating the software on a computer. In fact, what the standards require is a massive investment in *learning,* not in installation or implementation. Learning requires patience, repetition, practice, feedback, and above all, a forgiving, psychologically safe environment in which problems and mistakes are our friends because they teach us what not to do the next time.

Real professions have ways of dealing with this kind of learning efficiently and directly. My brother-in-law is an orthopedic surgeon who has been in practice for nearly twenty years. Over this period he has had to change his surgical practice fundamentally—some would say radically—at least three times. He entered the field when orthopedic surgery still required relatively traumatic and invasive intervention; he now does virtually everything with fiber optics and an incision that barely requires stitches. At each juncture in this transformation of his practice, he has had to unlearn a previous practice, learn how to do something he did not previously know how to do—using protocols and instruments that previously did not exist, with a high level of fluency and proficiency—and eventually pass a series of assessments that certified him for relicensure. All this occurred in an environment in which his practice was totally transparent to his colleagues (he has to submit video of his surgical procedures as a condition of relicensure), under the scrutiny of his peers. The medical profession would not think of raising the standards for surgical practice without concurrently creating the institutional conditions under which the learning that would support those practices could occur. Yet in education we routinely change the ground rules for practice and, with the wave of a hand, ask teachers to engage students in practices of learning that they themselves have never experienced as learners. And then we wonder why our best efforts at reform have such mixed results.

A fundamental principle of professional learning is something I have come to call "Elmore's Second Law":[i] The impact of professional

---

[i]For those who are interested, "Elmore's First Law" is this: In classrooms, students generally learn what they are taught; if it hasn't been learned, it probably hasn't been taught.

development on teacher practice and student learning is inverse to the square of its distance from the classroom. Learning through observation and analysis of instructional practice that is physically located in the classroom results in an experience in which the practitioner-learner's physical experience "registers" in the brain as a complex connection between what the eye sees, what the observer feels about what the eye sees, and how the observer "makes sense" of the connection between what is observed and what is felt. The experience is immediate, and it registers with an affective response, which increases the likelihood that the experience will be available for later use in analysis and practice. When the practitioner-learner is a more-or-less passive consumer of the experience—say, sitting in a conference room or a large hall, listening to an expert talk about instructional practice—the "learning" registers in the brain as a series of images that require little or no active sense-making, and little or no affective response, reducing markedly the likelihood that it will be available for later use. This type of experience is more about vicarious entertainment than about learning. Physicians and medical educators have intuitively mastered the principle of connecting head work and hand work for generations. As medical education has developed in recent decades, most medical schools have tightened the connection between the "medical science" part of the curriculum and the "medical practice" part, putting students in situations throughout their medical training where they have to learn to move back and forth between classroom instruction and active problem solving in clinical settings, increasing retention and application.

What Vivian Troen and Kitty Boles have done in this book is to bring this model of professional learning directly into the world of teacher practice. As the authors note, there are now many books that develop and elaborate models of rounds practice in various settings—system-level, school-level, cross-role, and so on—but none that deal directly with the use of rounds as a dedicated learning environment for teachers. This book provides the scaffolding and support that teachers can use, on their own or in an organized fashion, as part of a more systemic strategy, to create the infrastructure necessary to bring collective learning deliberately and explicitly into the daily life of teachers.

Troen and Boles stress in many places in this book the importance of rounds as a culture-building practice. For me, this is the central contribution they make. Rounds is not simply a practice; it is a practice in the service of building a professional culture. Among the important dimensions of this culture-building activity is, first, the deliberate acknowledgement that "problems are our friends." Instructional practice advances by identifying and acknowledging that problems exist in the way we do our work, by unflinchingly calling them problems, and by collectively engaging in practices that surface and address these problems. Second, professional learning requires practitioner-learners to "depersonalize" problems and practices by creating a body of descriptive evidence and developing ways of talking about them that stimulate productive problem solving, and then "repersonalizing" them by making binding commitments to learn new modes of practice. Third, learning is both an individual and a social activity. Mastery of complex instructional practices requires high individual investment in learning, but it also requires high social support and psychological safety in the learning environment. These are only three of the many ways in which the practice of rounds leads to the transformation of the culture of professional learning. The important message is that to engage in the practice without the intention of transforming the culture is to lose the benefit of the practice. This book is a powerful guide to the future of professional learning for teachers.

Preface

This book is about facilitating the process of teachers' engaging in the professional practice of something we call "Teacher Rounds." As we define it, Teacher Rounds (sometimes called Faculty Rounds, or simply Rounds) is a model in which teachers themselves direct their own course of learning through observation and analysis to improve their students' learning.

Our idea of teachers doing rounds is not new. As early as 1988, the two of us, as part of a school–college collaboration to improve teacher preparation, began experimenting in a few Boston-area schools with something we called "grand rounds," based on the model of medical school training.[1] We began grand rounds with an emphasis on the training of teacher interns, who signed up to participate three times a month.

During grand rounds, teachers taught individual lessons while interns and other teachers observed. The group subsequently examined and analyzed the lesson. Through grand rounds, more experienced practitioners passed on knowledge and experience to the less experienced. Grand rounds encouraged teachers to observe, discuss, and analyze teaching, which, in turn, allowed them to create strategies to improve their own teaching.

Grand rounds served several purposes. Perhaps most important, it institutionalized and perpetuated the norm of "teaching as a public act." It also gave teachers an ongoing set of opportunities to observe and learn from other teachers, to reflect on their own practice, and to become further "encultured" in a community where everyone participates in the dual acts of teaching and learning. Experienced teachers reported that their own practice was positively affected in ways they had not anticipated, and they wanted grand rounds to expand so that more of them could participate more fully. A research study conducted by a classroom teacher in one of the schools revealed how powerful an effect grand rounds was having on the participating teachers. It was our belief then, and still is, that transforming teaching from a private to a public act is critical to education reform.

Our work during that period led us to the belief that teachers working in teams could help assist in that goal and that, while teachers often collaborated on projects or events or met to solve problems of logistics, teacher teams rarely truly collaborated on improving instruction. Research and consulting in the area of teacher teams brought us to the development and refinement of strategies to improve the effectiveness of teacher teams. In our book on teacher teams,[2] rounds is briefly discussed as a strategy for improving instructional practice; as we completed that book, we realized that the subject of rounds needed a larger discussion, perhaps apart from the context of teacher teams—hence, the impetus for this book.

We must point out that ours is not the only model for rounds; others exist that differ in their approach to solving the problems of improving learning for teachers and students alike.

First and foremost among the different approaches is the groundbreaking book *Instructional Rounds in Education*,[3] which continues to inform and enrich our work. Instructional rounds is, as the subtitle of that book declares, a network approach to improving teaching and learning, involving higher-level educators and policymakers such as principals, deputy superintendents, superintendents, district curriculum directors, union representatives, and in many cases, teachers. We owe a great deal to the many concepts expressed by the creators of that model, which has been influential in our work with teachers in the teaching and implementation of rounds. These concepts include an understanding of the importance of the instructional core and choosing a common problem of practice, as well as the approach to observation that the *Instructional Rounds* authors call "learning to see, unlearning to judge."

In the years since its publication, the idea of *Instructional Rounds*, like any excellent idea, has evolved into practices that use different formats and approaches to reach the common purpose of instructional and organizational improvement. In addition to the network-based, cross-site rounds practice described in the 2009 book, many schools and school systems have developed school-based rounds approaches, which can be much more frequent, involve many more teachers, and bring improvement practices closer to classrooms.[4]

As presented here in *The Power of Teacher Rounds*, our model of rounds can be team specific, responding to a problem of practice that is directly related to the issues of one team. Teacher Rounds is a vibrant subset of the different ways to bring rounds closer to teachers; its focus on the classroom is its "comparative advantage." Teacher Rounds is not about district change. It is concrete and situated close to practice; however, Rounds can also connect directly to an entire school's problem of practice and become part of the school's improvement plan.

In *The Power of Teacher Rounds* we present a hands-on, step-by-step guide designed to assist the facilitators of rounds as they engage in the process. We offer it with the hope that it will give Teacher Rounds facilitators, as well as others faced with the challenges presented by rounds implementation, the tools to reach our common goal—the improvement of teaching and learning.

Acknowledgments

In classrooms all over America, there are silent heroes who take risks opening up their practice to public view—risks unthought of just a decade or two ago—to improve their practice and give students the benefit of better teaching. If we've learned anything in the 30-plus years we've been teaching, observing, mentoring, and coaching, it is that classroom teachers want nothing more than to see their students succeed. And for that, they put themselves on the line.

Many others behind the front lines are willing to put in the thought, energy, and hard work to help teachers achieve their dreams of success. In that spirit, we'd like to acknowledge those who helped us along the long road leading up to the development of this book.

We begin by remembering our teaching days at the Edward Devotion Elementary School in Brookline, Massachusetts, in the early 1980s. There we found teachers and school leaders who joined us in the struggle to develop the tools and techniques of teachers working in teams, which led, ultimately, to our group tinkering around the edges of a practice we came to call "Rounds." We were supported by our fearless, indomitable, and always encouraging principal, Jerry Kaplan, and Devotion's cadre of excellent teachers, including Gretchen Albertini, Steve Brady, Jack DeLong, Martha Farlow, Nancy Frane, Bill Gardner, Betsy Kellogg, Betsy Lake, Jim Swaim, and the late Joanne Rostler.

Through the years, our work has been informed by the wise counsel and constructive criticism and support of Karen Worth, the professor at Wheelock College who gave generously of her time and talents to examine closely the manuscript of this book, and found numerous ways to improve and refine our ideas and methods. It was Karen who three decades ago provided the inspiration for our creating together a school–college partnership that became one of the first Professional Development Schools in the country.

The wisdom and vision of Richard Elmore, who generously offered once again to write a foreword for us, inform our work and permeate this book. His ideas inspire us daily.

We owe much of what we have learned about Rounds to the generosity of Marc Baker, the brilliant and tireless head of school at Gann Academy in Waltham, Massachusetts, who gave us space (literally and figuratively) and the connections to build an infrastructure of Rounds groups at Gann, and found the funding to support that work. It was also at Gann that we met and came to appreciate the fine minds and skilled leadership qualities of our contributors, Aviva Scheur and Jacob Pinnolis, who were the "thought partners" that made the success of Rounds possible at Gann. Their deep thinking and commitment to the idea that Rounds could have a significant impact on school culture made an incalculable difference in the development of Rounds as a practice to improve teaching and learning. Working collaboratively with the school's fine teachers and department chairs, they created a working "Rounds laboratory" at Gann that led to the kind of schoolwide improvement rarely seen in other schools. We must acknowledge the support and wisdom of Susie Tanchel, then associate head of school at Gann, and Gann board member Leo Sprecher, who provided funding assistance and never settled for anything less than the best of ideas or concepts.

We value the many contributions made by Sharon-Feiman Nemser, director of the Jack, Joseph and Morton Mandel Center for Studies in Jewish Education at Brandeis University and a valued friend and colleague who has, over the years, generously critiqued our work, shared her expertise, and deepened our thinking on mentoring, teacher preparation, and professional learning communities. We greatly appreciate that the background research for our book was in part supported by the Jack, Joseph and Morton Mandel Center for Studies in Jewish Education at Brandeis, a partnership between Brandeis University and the Mandel Foundation. We also wish to thank the staff of the Mandel Center—Liz DiNolfo, Galit Higgins, and Susanne Shavelson—for their valuable assistance.

We thank Tom DelPrete at Clark University for his many writings and deep understanding of Instructional Rounds, and for the informative conversations we've had with him about preservice and in-service teachers.

Our friend and colleague Barbara Neufeld, president and founder of Education Matters, has, for more than 20 years, made an indelible mark on our work as teachers and consultants, and her expertise in a broad range of matters has . . . mattered.

Joellen Killion, senior advisor at Learning Forward, has been our cheerleader for years—always helping us get our ideas out to the larger world through various venues. Her kindness and willingness to go out of her way for us have sustained us in many ways.

We owe much to the inimitable and indispensable Dan Alpert, our acquisitions editor at Corwin, who most clearly understood our vision with *The Power of Teacher Teams* and was eager to encourage us with this book on Rounds. He guided us around missteps with our original book proposal and helped clarify our concepts and ideas along the way. He gave us his frank and detailed comments—critical when he needed to be and supportive at all times. He is every writer's dream editor.

And we would be greatly remiss if we did not acknowledge the work of an often unsung hero, the production editor—in our case, it was Libby Larson for our last book, and we are grateful that she was available to work with us on this one as well. Her superhuman, scrupulous attention to detail was always unflagging. Our thanks also to Meg Granger, our Corwin copy editor, for her skillful handling of our manuscript.

Colleague Francesca Stark, prodigious worker and highly respected 5th-grade teacher at the K–8 Michael Driscoll School in Boston, has been a friend and valued sounding board since arriving on our scene as Vivian's teacher intern more than 20 years ago. Since then, she has outpaced us in her wisdom and deep insights about teacher–student interactions. Not incidentally, she also provided inspiration and perspiration for our last book.

A supremely dedicated principal, Traci A. Griffith of the Eliot K–8 School in Boston, presented the concept of Rounds to her teachers and then arranged for us to work with her 3rd- and 4th-grade team. We wish to thank those teachers who collaborated with us and who took the risk of being videoed, knowing full well that their practice would be visible to an outside audience.

Our profound thanks go to Shimon Waronker, the founder of the New American Academies in New York City. Taking inspiration from the ideas expressed in our book *Who's Teaching Your Children?*, Shimon brought his own brilliant vision of how public elementary schools could be structured to the chancellor of the New York City Public Schools and, when he founded his first New American Academy, graciously invited us into that school. Later, Pepe Gutierrez, principal of the Bronx New American Academy, and Master Teacher Keisha

Green enthusiastically welcomed us into their school and gave us the opportunity to work with an excellent 2nd-grade team of teachers. We are grateful to those teachers, whose deep thought and eagerness to improve the lives and learning of the children in their school shone through their work, their conversations with us, and their dedication to Teacher Rounds.

Our appreciation to Jane Cohen, who in early days, as head of school at the South Area Solomon Schechter School in Stoughton, Massachusetts, allowed us wide latitude in experimenting with Rounds and continues to provide counsel from her work on teacher learning at Yeshiva University. Shira Horowitz, also at SASS at the time, was an early believer and, better than that, an early adopter who not only courageously videoed her own practice as a host teacher but then made her video available at education conferences to spread a greater understanding of Rounds among audiences of teachers and administrators.

Talented and tireless English teacher Charles Shyrock IV, who started a Rounds group at Bishop McNamara High School in Forestville, Maryland, generously gave us his excellent video on choosing a problem of practice. We received help and support for other videos that appear in this book from those who work at the Harvard Graduate School of Education's Information Technology Center, especially Susan Geddis Eppling. Harvard student and video editor Peter Kirschmann worked long hours on our videos, and master's students Elizabeth Barkay, Tracy Miller, and Karen Taylor provided energy and valuable insights as they worked with us. We thank them all.

Barney Brawer, Kitty's husband, needs special recognition for his contributions of patience and steadiness throughout the process of developing this book, and for giving Kitty invaluable advice drawn from his own experience as a Boston school principal.

And last, we owe an enormous debt of gratitude to Vivian's husband, Paul Wesel, who throughout our more than 30 years of collaboration on dozens of speeches, presentations, articles, and three books has been even more than a text editor, researcher, materials organizer, ideas tester, schedule keeper, coffee provider, and energy inducer—he has been a dear friend and ever-supportive fan and champion. Paul is a stalwart, level-headed counselor and a wise colleague, and we believe it is fair to say that without his many and varied contributions, this book would likely never have come into being.

Publisher's Acknowledgments

Corwin gratefully acknowledges the contributions of the following reviewers:

Janice Bradley, assistant professor

Jenni Donohoo, research consultant and staff developer

Victoria Duff, senior consultant

Lanelle Gordin, educator

Linda Munger, senior consultant for Learning Forward Center for Results

James L. Roussin, educational consultant

Andrew F. Szczepaniak, district administrator

Jennifer York-Barr, professor

Introduction

Getting From Then to Now

Want to know what's happening with education in America? Well, everything . . . and nothing. That is to say, while education reform initiatives regularly come and go, we seem to be stuck with a model of education that dates back to the 19th century, with its culture of personal rather than shared accountability. This is a model that stubbornly resists substantial improvements, with schools populated by teachers and school leaders who are not taught the basic skills, knowledge, and value of collaboration but are nonetheless increasingly called on to form teams, join groups, and mentor others.[5]

We believe that for school improvement to take place—meaning improvements in teaching and learning—there must be opportunities for teachers to move from an increasingly archaic model of individual responsibility to a more collaborative model of collective responsibility.

Consider this: In the three decades since publication of the education survey *A Nation at Risk*, there have been extensive changes to education policy—standards-based reform, pay for performance, No Child Left Behind, Race to the Top, more testing, more evaluation, charter schools. And yet nothing seems to work. Today, 1 in 4 Americans fails to earn a high school diploma on time, and the United States lags behind other countries in the percentage of young people who complete college. Former education secretary William Bennett puts it bluntly: "If there's a bottom line, it's that we're spending twice as much money on education as we did in 1983 and the results haven't changed all that much."[6]

Despite significant efforts and hundreds of millions of dollars spent on "improvements," we have little to show. Why? It is our position that in the perpetual scramble to improve the education of children, a critical component of education reform has almost always

1

been ignored, no matter what reforms have been created. The component of *collaboration* is the missing ingredient in the preparation of teachers, which is vital to the success of meeting those reforms. And now, we have something called the Common Core State Standards. This broadly comprehensive initiative shows great promise, but its implementation is already proving to be an enormous challenge.

Implementing the Common Core State Standards

Will the Common Core State Standards move us beyond *A Nation at Risk?* Not unless we help teachers by giving them the understanding and support they need to implement them. We would suggest that what is most needed is a conceptual change among educators at all levels. That is the fundamental philosophy behind these standards: a move away from the belief that imparting and memorizing information is the primary goal of classroom teaching and toward the understanding that what's important is *making sense* of that information.

A common question among teachers is, *What do my students need to know and be able to do?* Teachers may arrive at their answers in a number of different ways. But most often the missing second question is, *What do I, as their teacher, need to know and be able to do?*

That's where Teacher Rounds comes in, because Teacher Rounds is a low-cost, high-impact strategy and a powerful tool for implementing the Common Core State Standards.

Basic Ideas About Teacher Rounds

Throughout this book, we will most often refer to Teacher Rounds simply as Rounds, or sometimes Faculty Rounds. This is to distinguish rounds conducted by teachers from instructional rounds,[7] which may be conducted, for example, by members of interschool networks consisting of principals, union representatives, district administrators, superintendents, and often teachers.

Teacher Rounds

- creates a framework for critical colleagueship;
- builds norms for collaboration;
- supports and assists veteran teachers, as well as the less experienced;
- reduces isolation and promotes collaboration;

- helps develop a shared vision of good teaching;
- makes student learning the focus of the group;
- provides a venue for problem solving; and
- facilitates the sharing of successful practice.

A word here about what is meant by "critical colleagueship": A model for critical colleagueship[8] specifies three norms that should be reflected in teacher talk and exchange if the professional learning community is to reflect growth and student learning.[9]

1. Teachers need to be open to discussing conflict and expressing different views about teaching. This conflict, if it is useful, is "productive disequilibrium."

2. Teachers need to become increasingly familiar (and comfortable) with ambiguity.

3. Given the open conflict and ambiguity that, it is hoped, will strengthen and not weaken community, teachers must seek a collective commitment to continue their work together amidst the ambiguity and conflict.

About This Book

The chapter headings are fairly self-explanatory, and a quick read will reveal the *what, why, who,* and *how* of implementing Teacher Rounds. Inside the chapters, however, things can get somewhat more complex. If the theoretical and practical sometimes seem to collide in workshops, activities, diagrams, cases, tables, worksheets, videos, cases, and guides to case analysis . . . well, there is a method to the layers of interwoven ideas and concepts and—stick with us—it will all begin to make sense once you absorb the basics and start putting some of the tools and planning into action.

This is a guidebook, designed to make available and accessible lots of different components, at different times and for different purposes. But it does come with a warning label:

Significant and lasting change can happen only over time, with persistence and work.

The good news is, we have seen how Rounds can transform teachers' lives and improve their practice. We know it can be done, and this book is a compendium of those learnings and strategies acquired in the process of helping Rounds groups become successful. So dig in.

PART I

Background

1

What Is
Teacher Rounds?

Teacher Rounds Is a Unique
Form of Professional Learning

Most people are familiar with the medical practice of "doing rounds," in which interns and mentoring physicians visit patients in an institutional setting, observe patients' various conditions, and later discuss their observations and analyze possible treatment options and outcomes. In the medical profession, doing rounds is viewed as a significant and highly important form of *professional learning.*

While rounds for physicians and rounds for teachers are not precisely the same, the comparison is a shortcut way to begin thinking about what constitutes this kind of *school-based* professional learning.

What distinguishes a Round from other professional development is that it occurs in the actual context of teaching and learning, it draws on and encourages investigation and reflection on teachers' and learners' experience, it provides a shared experience as a basis for conversation, and it brings to bear interactively the different perspectives and expertise of different participants in the reflection process. Its meaningfulness lies in the collaborative way in which it involves teachers as professional and adult learners, and particularly in its direct relation to teachers' experience and practice and, in turn, to the children to whom teachers are dedicated. It builds professional development community through processes of inquiry and reflection.[1]

Here might be an appropriate place to talk about the terms *professional development* and *professional learning*. The term *professional development* has been used for decades in discussions of ongoing teacher education. However, it seems to us that the term has lost some of its currency and is being replaced by *professional learning*, which we prefer and have tried to use consistently throughout this book.

In any event, in terms of professional learning for teachers, Rounds groups require explicit knowledge and skill, training in areas such as planning and facilitating productive meetings, learning to observe and use data, building consensus, and providing growth-producing feedback to teachers. Essentially, Teacher Rounds is a feedback system in which the feedback is information about what teachers actually accomplished compared with what they attempted to do, related to student learning. The hoped-for result is that teachers can then, in a collaborative fashion, analyze the observations and make changes in their individual practice.

Rounds is . . .	*Rounds is not . . .*[a]
A practice designed to support an existing improvement strategy at the school or system level	A program
A practice that is iterative and woven into existing improvement processes	An event
Focused on the practice of people, to learn about effective learning and teaching	An evaluation tool or an assessment of individual teachers or schools
Focused on patterns of practice (learning and teaching) and predicted results	An implementation check or a compliance with directives
Focused on collective learning rather than individual supervisory practice, on moving the organization forward	Training for supervision
A community of practice in which teachers push one another and learn from one another	Passive

[a]Adapted and used with permission of Lee Teitel, lecturer at the Harvard Graduate School of Education.

A Rounds Group in Action: A True-to-Life Story

The following is an account of teachers collaborating in a high school Rounds group, told here to provide an inside view of how a Rounds group works in real life. It reflects our experiences in several schools where we have coached, observed, and studied actual Rounds groups in action. While the school and the teachers are fictional, their story is not.

> Understanding Rounds as both a linear and circular process takes patience, study, and reflection. As you follow this story, it will be helpful to refer to those sections referenced throughout the book that illuminate and describe more fully the situations and experiences mentioned here.

Pre-Rounds Meeting: Choosing a Compelling Problem of Practice[2]

It is the first week in September. In a conference room at Everett Salton High School, eight teachers sit around a conference table and settle in after unpacking notebooks and laptops, and exchanging brief greetings and small talk. With the exception of one teacher new to the process, teachers in this group have already experienced one full year of Rounds and they all know the drill.

Salton High has 1,100 students and 85 teachers; the school has just begun its second year of Rounds. There are about 40 teachers in the five Rounds groups, but this will change from year to year, and Rounds groups will not, in all likelihood, be composed of the same teachers each year. Drawn from all departments, the teachers come into Rounds groups based on schedules that match with back-to-back planning periods. These periods allow time for the 1½-hour Rounds meetings held once a month.

To join a Rounds group, a teacher is required to have at least 2 years of classroom teaching experience. Participation in Rounds groups is designed to offer teachers an opportunity to attain a higher level of professional growth and development, improve their practice, gain deeper insights into their teaching, and, most important, improve their students' performance.

Acting in her capacity as the group's facilitator, Glenda Solas, a veteran teacher in the Humanities Department, officially opens the meeting by welcoming to the group the third-year science teacher, Gasper Marchand. Gasper has not yet participated in Rounds, but Glenda prepped him in the Rounds process prior to this meeting.

After being introduced to the teachers, a few of whom he already knows, Gasper says,

I've really been looking forward to joining a Rounds group. Last year I talked to teachers in a few of the other Rounds groups, and they all had positive things to say about the experience. Some had their struggles, of course—which is only natural—but at the end of the year they saw positive changes in their practice, and they were comfortable with being observed and getting feedback, which they told me was enormously helpful. They were incredibly enthusiastic when they talked about the opportunity to discuss their practice with teachers in other disciplines. The chance for a math teacher to observe how an English teacher engages in solving problems of practice common to both teachers must be an amazing experience. So thank you . . . I'm glad to be here.

At Salton High, Rounds group facilitators are selected by the principal, but different schools follow other methods for this process. Facilitators can be selected by a professional development director, a teacher leader, or the group itself. The job of facilitator is a difficult one that requires a great deal of experience and skill (which is the reason for this book).

Here, it may be instructive to pause and consider what this Rounds group already knows and is able to do. Last year, every teacher who joined a Rounds group first had to participate in a process of preparation and induction. All members participated in a brief workshop on classroom observation and reviewed the "working protocols," which included a worksheet to guide classroom observations, a debriefing protocol, a worksheet for preparing records of practice, and the ground rules for observation. The group also had to develop a set of group norms. A new set of group norms is developed or revised during the year's first meeting, and the group's norms are revisited at each subsequent meeting to "check in." This experience is completely new to Gasper. He knows he has to quickly get up to speed, but he also knows he'll have the full mentoring and assistance of the facilitator.

After revising the norms, the next order of business is for the group to identify a singular, compelling *problem of practice* that will be the focus of the group's energies, study, and engagement over the entire academic year. Fully aware of the impact of the Common Core State Standards (CCSS), a subject of much discussion last year, group members understand that their problem of practice needs to be aligned with CCSS.

After serious and lively discussion, facilitated by Glenda, the teachers take this as their problem of practice:

Teachers do not regularly facilitate critical thinking among and between students to make the subject matter meaningful.

This problem of practice is aligned to the CCSS Speaking and Listening Standards for Grades 6 through 12: "Initiate and participate effectively in a range of collaborative discussions (one-on-one, in groups, and teacher-led) with diverse partners, building on others' ideas and expressing their own clearly and persuasively" (see Appendix A).

Now the members of the group go even further. They refer to CCSS to look for guiding questions that will help them focus on their problem of practice, by asking,
How can we

- *encourage all students to ask critical questions and consider diverse perspectives about subject matter?*
- *help students analyze and draw valid conclusions about content being learned?*
- *provide opportunities for students to think, discuss, interact, reflect, and evaluate content?*
- *provide opportunities for students to learn and practice skills in meaningful contexts?*
- *encourage students to take intellectual risks, to ask probing questions that will more fully engage them in grappling with the intellectual work of the subject matter?*

The group's next order of business is to schedule observation of the host teacher's classroom.

Preparing the Host Teacher

For every Round, the teacher whose class is being observed is the "host teacher." Prior to the observation, the host teacher fills out a Host Teacher Preparation Form (see Figure 1.1), which provides information for observers to use during the observation.

It is the practice for facilitators to model being the first host teacher; so it's up to Glenda to get the ball rolling. She was a host teacher last year, has more experience as a result of collaborating with the other host teachers, and, since the teachers already trust her, can model how one teacher can help another complete the form. This simple move provides a safety net and a scaffold for the other teachers.

"Okay," she says, "let's get out our schedules and see when you can all observe my class."

The observation is set for the following Thursday, and Glenda says, "That's really good—the class will be discussing the political dominance of Caesar Augustus. I'll be filling out my Host Teacher

Preparation Form and e-mailing it to each of you by the end of the week."

To help focus the Round, please fill out this form and e-mail to your Rounds group.

Name _____   **Date of Round** _____

1. **Review/explain problem of practice.**

2. **Provide context for the lesson.**
   - What is the task?

   - What is your role as the teacher?

   - What are the students going to be doing?

3. **On what should the observers focus their attention?**

4. **To what extent should/would you like observers to interact with students?**

"Now, while we're here," Glenda continues, "let's confirm the date for the observation debrief meeting. Luckily, this year all the debrief meetings are in the master schedule."

In subsequent Rounds, Glenda will meet separately with each host teacher to help prepare for having his or her class observed by the Rounds group. During the year, each teacher in the group will be a host teacher, and with eight members in the group, the numbers work out so that every teacher will have an opportunity to host at least once.

Realistically, Glenda knows that no host teacher can fill out the Host Teacher Preparation Form alone. Understanding this, and since she has no facilitator to be her guide, she reaches out to a facilitator from another Rounds group in the school. They decide to meet over lunch and support each other in completing their Host Teacher Preparation Forms. This move will become the model for future facilitators at Salton High.

Glenda is ready with a problem she needs to solve, and she shares it with the facilitator from the other Rounds group: Glenda is preparing a lesson on Caesar Augustus. In the past, she has had difficulty moving her students beyond the basic facts to a deeper understanding of this pivotal leader's actions and prominence. She worries that her students do not grapple in any meaningful way with the issues presented in this lesson, and she wonders how to encourage greater student ownership of the material so their own critical engagement will enhance their learning.

With this problem in mind, she prepares her Host Teacher Preparation Form and e-mails it to the other members of the group, along with their Observation Worksheets, in preparation for her classroom observation.

Observing the Host Teacher

With her Host Teacher Preparation Form (see Appendix B), Glenda has outlined her lesson, providing the group with background and context for the lesson, which is to be part of a continuing historical analysis of Caesar Augustus and the period in which he ruled. She has laid out her teaching goals, given the group a detailed explanation of her lesson, and offered some guidance about where she wants the group to focus their attention.

The next Thursday, seven teachers walk into Glenda's third-period 10th-grade history class. With computers, worksheets, and notebooks in hand, the teachers are ready for their observation. Video equipment has been set up to record the lesson for later viewing by the host teacher or other teachers who might want to see the lesson again prior to the debrief meeting scheduled for the following week.

Teachers try to attend classroom observations in person, but this is not always possible; not all teachers can get coverage. At Salton High, teachers are able to observe the class on video, since it is posted online (just for the group) immediately after the class. They have all agreed to follow the ground rules for observation (see Figure 1.2) and to record observations on their observation worksheets (see Figure 1.3).

Figure 1.2   Ground Rules for Observing Rounds

- Observers are silent during the lesson; no side conversations.
- Observers remain in the classroom during the entire lesson.
- Observers will circulate freely when students are working individually or in groups, and move to the side or back of the room during whole-class discussions.
- Observers are encouraged to ask students questions about the lesson when appropriate, with permission of host teacher. They refrain from teaching or assisting students.
- Observers make notes on individual student comments and conversations, noting the names of students, if possible. They may also use a seating chart to map student responses.
- Observers record examples of how students construct their understanding through the discussion and activities.

Figure 1.3   Rounds Observation Worksheet

Teacher _____   Date _____

Problem of Practice _____

Teacher actions, quotes	Student names, actions, quotes	Questions/analyses

Debriefing the Observation

This is the once-a-month meeting of the whole Rounds group. They will meet again next month, after another classroom observation hosted by another teacher, in a monthly cycle that continues throughout the school year. At each meeting, a Rounds group member will volunteer to be the next host teacher.

The debrief meeting begins with Glenda, as host teacher, reviewing her goals for the lesson, reflecting on strategies she used to address the problem of practice, and considering the ongoing challenges she faces when she tries to have her students do more of the intellectual work. She indicates that she is looking forward to using this meeting to get more specifics about what teachers observed during the round.

Glenda reminds the teachers to review their notes on their observations, make connections on how what they observed relates to the group's problem of practice, and focus on how the lesson attempted to address that specific problem.

Using the Rounds Debriefing Protocol (see Figure 1.4) to guide this meeting, the teachers describe what they saw during the lesson, what they wondered as they were watching the lesson, and something they learned from the observation. Here are a few examples from the debrief of Glenda's lesson. (Step 1 of the regular debriefing protocol, "Honoring Commitments," is omitted from this first meeting but is used in all subsequent Rounds meetings.)

Some Observations

Eager to show his enthusiasm for participation, Gasper jumps in with the first observation: "Your use of group work was terrific, and the kids got so much done in a short period of time."

Glenda interrupts, "I need to step out of my role as host teacher and put on my facilitator's hat. It's really important during this section that we focus on giving data—just the facts, rather than an opinion. Sometimes it's hard to make that distinction. Like, what does 'terrific' mean? What data do you have that means 'terrific' to you? And what does a 'short period of time' mean to you? How long? What did they accomplish? Sorry, Gasper, but this is such an important aspect of Rounds I felt I had to interrupt."

The observations continue.

"The way you structure group work—you break it down for students," offers Andrea Grosky, a sixth-year math teacher, " a little bit of group work, then the whole class . . . then group work again."

Figure 1.4   Rounds Debriefing Protocol

(1 hr., 15 mins.)

1. **Honoring Commitments**

   Review briefly what you have done since the previous month's meeting, and share records of practice showing evidence of that commitment. (15 mins.)

2. **Sharing Observations**

   a. Host teacher reflects on the lesson, explains what his or her goals were for addressing the problem of practice and in what ways goals were or were not met, and shares data on what students learned. (2 mins.)
   b. All observers take a few minutes to review notes and jot down specifics on the lesson, focusing on how the lesson attempted to address the problem of practice. (2 mins.)
   c. Observers share data from observation. What did you **see**? Use *descriptive data* only, not inferences or judgments. (10 mins.)

3. **Wonderings/Open, Honest Questions**

   What do you genuinely wonder about in what you saw in observation? These are open, honest questions. The questions should not have preambles, they should not be disguised advice, and you should not have a particular answer in mind. The point is not to offer solutions but to stimulate thinking. (10 mins.)

4. **Selective Response by Host Teacher**

   Respond to what seems most relevant to the problem of practice, extend a wondering, and so on (3 mins.)

5. **Learnings**

   Each person will describe something he or she has learned from the observation and debrief. (10 mins.)

6. **Commitments**

   How will you modify your instruction based on what was learned during the observation and debrief? (10 mins.)

7. **Developing a Plan to Experiment**

   Teachers develop a plan to experiment with modifying their practice prior to the next Round. (5 mins.)

Science teacher Alan Faulk talks about his observations of Glenda's lesson: "You had a sheet for students to look at and told them to use it to help guide the discussion."

From English teacher Patricia Menendez: "You gave students opportunities to lead a discussion and teach . . . and you did not comment on what they said. I kept track of how much you talked and how much the kids talked. I can show you my table."

Some Wonderings

"I noticed that after two particular questions, it was clear that you wanted all the kids to answer in unison. How did you signal students that that's what you wanted?" wonders Lillian Liu.

"I'm wondering," says Shira Kaplan, "if it wouldn't be better to put the analysis in the beginning of the lesson if, in fact, that was the essence of the lesson."

Glenda makes a timeout gesture with her hands and says, "Sorry, I need to become facilitator again. Would someone volunteer to help Shira reframe that comment into a wondering?"

Tentatively, Helene Morris responds with this wondering about the structuring of the lesson: "I know you wanted to introduce the idea of analysis to the students, but I was wondering why analysis came quite late in the lesson."

Glenda asks the group what they think: "Is that a wondering?"

Shira admits, "This is very challenging for me."

Alan continues the wonderings: "In the beginning part of the class, there seemed to be a sluggish response to your questions, with how students raised their hands—their body language—and I was wondering if there was a way to check for their understanding of the questions . . . was there another way to get more participation."

Some Learnings

Jerry Belzer reflects on his own practice: "What I learned was that I have to ask myself what it means for different students in my class to have periods of silence where they don't participate—what are they thinking when they don't answer my questions? I learned that I need strategies to encourage a student to ask a question relevant to the other students."

"I noticed how energetic a recitation could be—kids were answering energetically—and it made me feel good about recitation as a style. . . . I thought to myself, I would really like to have more tools for handling a recitation when there is less participation," says Gasper.

"I thought there was a little too much recitation, actually," admits Glenda, "but I felt bound by the amount of reading we had to slog through. The kids had never read this historian before and they had never read a primary source from this period. . . . My learning is that I have to rethink the curriculum changes that the department made last summer."

Committing to a Change of Practice

As the meeting draws to a close, the teachers make a commitment to alter their practice in some way based on what they have seen and discussed.

Lillian begins, "I'm going to try something to get students to participate more—maybe start by asking clarifying questions only and then have other kids answer the questions . . . allow kids to give more and take stage away from me. I'm not sure what the record of practice would look like. Any ideas?"

Two teachers suggest ways to develop a problem of practice.

"You could keep track of your questions and then record who answers what. Recording will also help you talk less," quips Alan. "After you've done that a few times, you could video a discussion and track the amount of time you talk and when the kids talk."

Helen offers, "You might want to target a few of the quiet students and measure how this intervention affects their participation."

"I like to do a summary at the end of the class, but I often run out of time," says Jerry. "I'm going to try some other way to get data—written data would be best. . . . I'm going to commit to setting a timer to give me 5 minutes at the end of class for students to fill out 'exit cards' based on a question I put up on the board. Even if I can only do this once or twice a week, that would be an improvement."

Andrea expresses her desire to get a better read on what her students actually learned—or thought they learned—during a lesson "by asking students what they learned—what did they think we talked about today? I also have to ask myself what level of Bloom's taxonomy I was addressing. If students talk more about the 'what' rather than the synthesis, or analysis, I'll know my questions didn't generate the kind of thinking I wanted. If I ask more open-ended questions, will I get more open-ended answers back?"

Preparing for the Next Rounds Meeting: The Cycle Continues

At the end of this meeting, Jerry volunteers to be the next host teacher, and everyone takes out their schedules to select the best available time to observe Jerry's class. The period is selected to occur before (but not too much before) the already scheduled November Rounds debrief meeting.

Prior to Jerry's classroom observation, Glenda meets with him to help him work on his Host Teacher Preparation Form. Jerry then drafts his form and sends it to Glenda to review prior to the observation. Glenda suggests a few changes to clarify the focus of the observation and sends it back to Jerry, who then e-mails it to the group. The group observes Jerry's class, and 4 days later they hold their Rounds debrief meeting.

Sharing Records of Practice

There is an expectation that during the month, teachers will have experimented with the commitments they made during the meeting, documenting what they've done and how the students received their actions. They will each create what is called a record of practice (see Figure 1.5). To ensure that the previous month's records of practice are reviewed at the following Rounds group meeting, the Rounds Debriefing Protocol (refer back to Figure 1.4) begins with a section

Figure 1.5   Records of Practice for Rounds

Keeping track is a matter of reflective review and summarizing, in which there is both discrimination and record of the significant features of a developing experience. . . . It is the heart of intellectual organization and of the disciplined mind.

—John Dewey, *Experience and Education*

Records of practice—A record of practice is an artifact; it is something tangible from the realm of practice that can be studied by participants in the Rounds group.

We use artifacts to provide concrete evidence of changes made in teaching practice and student learning. This isn't about tracking progress but, rather, about tracking the *process* of changing our practice. When deciding on an artifact type, first consider the purpose of collecting the record of practice and the problem of practice you have in mind. Then you can determine the artifact that best fits that purpose and problem.

Examples:

- Lesson plan
- Discussion prompts
- Assessment
- Student work
- Teacher's journal
- Smart Board notes
- Video

labeled "Honoring Commitment," where teachers briefly share their records of practice, which have already been posted on Google Docs.

Teachers are asked to report on what they've tried in their classrooms between the last Round (when they made a commitment) and this Round. It is important to note that this is a challenging aspect of Rounds and it often takes several months before teachers are able to develop good records of practice. There generally isn't enough time to delve deeply into any one record, so only one or two teachers explain artifacts in detail.

At the debrief meeting in November, after the second round (this is the first time records of practice are shared), it is important for the facilitator to provide a well-developed artifact to model the process.

So at the November meeting, Glenda will present her record of practice (see Appendix C) in more detail. All the other teachers will also describe how they honored the commitments they made at the previous Rounds debrief meeting.

Twice a year, the group will devote an entire Rounds meeting to closely examining one record of practice from each teacher and appraising the student work that resulted from that change in practice. This deep review further strengthens and solidifies the yearly professional learning process of Rounds.

It's a Circular Path to Perfection

Every step of the Rounds process is a de facto commitment to take teachers' practice to the next level—to uncover more, learn more, do more. The whole purpose of Rounds is to enable a *change in teaching*, with this ultimate goal in mind: *IMPROVING STUDENT LEARNING.*

It is important to understand, at this stage, that a commitment to change practice is not a do-or-die effort, no turning back. It is, at first, an experiment. Facilitators will guide Rounds participants through what is often a trial-and-error process leading to frustration or success, or something in between. Some ideas work; some don't. Remarkably, that is one of the strengths of Rounds. If done well, Rounds provides a supportive environment in which risks are encouraged and results are shared by the group. Rounds is a continuous work in progress (see Figure 1.6). Improvements don't come easily or overnight, but when they do come, results can be significant and sustainable.

Figure 1.6   The Rounds Process

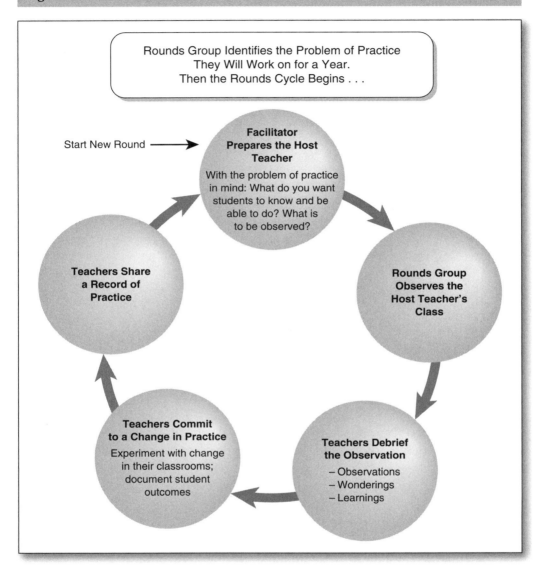

Rounds Group Identifies the Problem of Practice
They Will Work on for a Year.
Then the Rounds Cycle Begins . . .

Start New Round ⟶

**Facilitator
Prepares the Host
Teacher**

With the problem of practice
in mind: What do you want
students to know and be
able to do? What is
to be observed?

**Rounds Group
Observes the
Host Teacher's
Class**

**Teachers Share
a Record of
Practice**

**Teachers Commit
to a Change in Practice**

Experiment with change
in their classrooms;
document student
outcomes

**Teachers Debrief
the Observation**

– Observations
– Wonderings
– Learnings

2

Why Do Rounds?

Rounds Creates a Framework for Critical Colleagueship

Critical colleagueship is a professional development environment that helps teachers expose their classroom practices to other teachers and educators, and enables them to learn by unpacking authentic challenges teachers face and to think through plausible strategies.

Students are the beneficiaries when teacher learning is enriched by grounding professional development in the daily particulars of teacher practice. Meaningful teacher discussions around their practice, especially when situated within assumptions of critical collegiality, strengthen teacher-learning opportunities and reinforce the practical basis for teacher growth.[1] Teacher effectiveness is enhanced so that students benefit.

In a story about collaboration among medical doctors, reported in *The New York Times* science pages, 23 heart surgeons in Maine, New Hampshire, and Vermont agreed to observe one another regularly in the operating room and share their knowledge, insights, and approaches. Two years later, the death rate among their patients had fallen an astonishing 24%. Merely by emphasizing teamwork and communication instead of functioning as solitary practitioners, all the doctors had brought about significant changes in their individual and institutional practices.[2]

For teachers who, like heart surgeons, have traditionally worked as isolated professionals, the experience holds a powerful lesson. If our goal is to lower the "fatality rate" of young minds and see them thrive, it is obvious that we can do it better by collaborating in Rounds groups than by working alone.

Rounds Facilitates the Sharing of Successful Practice

Rounds promotes collaboration through the sharing of successful practice. Like doctors making hospital rounds and lawyers collaborating to provide feedback to their colleagues as they build a case, teachers in both public and independent schools have begun to purposefully probe the rich evidence at hand for what it can reveal about how teachers can better teach and students can better learn.

During Rounds, teachers teach an individual lesson while other teachers in their Rounds group observe. Through Rounds, more experienced practitioners can pass on knowledge and experience to the less experienced. There are opportunities for both veteran and less experienced teachers to learn, and those opportunities are encouraged. This is a model of Rounds practiced *by teachers, for teachers, and about teachers.* The teachers—one of whom is the facilitator—are in control of the entire process of observing, analyzing, learning, and making a strategic commitment to change their practice based on what they have learned.

Rounds Helps Develop a Shared Vision of Good Teaching

Rounds can be a vehicle to develop a common vision of good teaching by keeping track of interventions teachers make in their teaching as a result of commitments to changes in practice. (See "Developing a List of Common Criteria" in Chapter 5.)

This shared, explicit understanding of what good teaching looks like—of the ideal that all teachers in a school are striving for—provides an essential guide for new teacher learning. A shared vision of good teaching goes beyond a set of principles, such as "We value hands-on learning" or "Our school is child-centered." It describes the behaviors and dispositions of effective teachers: the ways in which they plan lessons, manage classrooms, present material, and relate to children, parents, and colleagues. This enables the school to create supports and learning experiences that help teachers develop those skills and knowledge to enhance student outcomes.

When the faculty of a school has a common vision for good teaching and colleagues are able to model and discuss that vision, new teachers have the opportunity to emulate and learn from them. In schools where there is no consistent vision of good teaching, new teachers receive confusing messages from colleagues and administrators about what they should be doing in their classrooms and what are the standards for success in that school.

Rounds Is a Low-Cost, High-Impact Strategy for Implementing the Common Core State Standards

In the wide world of education, professional opportunities for teachers to improve their practice are thin, sporadic, and of little use. According to Harvard University Professor Heather C. Hill, the "professional development 'system' for teachers is, by all accounts, broken."[3]

In contrast, collaboration and adult learning are at the heart of Rounds, and student learning is the lens through which teachers examine their practices. Well-implemented Rounds groups spread the culture of continual improvement to all classrooms. A spirit of collaboration is palpable, permeating hallway conversations, chance encounters in the parking lot or the lunchroom; conversations are ongoing and dedicated to promoting student learning. Rounds fulfills the principle that all teacher learning and development activities must be integrated with the day-to-day work of teaching and student learning, with standards guiding that work.

Our good friend and noted educator Roland Barth has commented, "[Collaboration] among the adults in the building has more impact on the quality and character of the school and the accomplishments of its youngsters than any other factor."

Publishing new standards will not by itself help our students become college or career ready; previous iterations of standards have historically failed to improve student learning. Traditional "sit-and-git" professional development endured by so many teachers merely reinforces the norm of increasing awareness and knowledge rather than focusing on implementation, sharing materials rather than identifying individual teaching challenges to expand teachers' expertise. So how will the Common Core State Standards (CCSS) become successful? Only with educators' capacity to make the *instructional shifts* that the standards require.[4] Teachers will have to learn to teach to these standards, and design lessons to guarantee rigor and cognitive demands to ensure that students are doing the intellectual work. Rounds has proven effective in empowering teachers to be in charge of the process by providing them with *tools and strategies to acquire and practice the skills necessary to achieve success in implementing CCSS.*

As a professional development strategy, hardly has there been an initiative with fewer added costs or burdens of extra time than Rounds. No outside consultants are needed. The role of facilitator fits neatly into the vision of teacher leader, which, in most cases, requires no extra salary than that already budgeted. Time for Rounds is already allocated on the master schedule for planning periods and professional development. And few would argue that when teachers make a commitment to change their practice and internally assess the value of their work as it affects student learning, the impact is a win–win.

Rounds Is Aligned With Learning Forward's Standards for Professional Learning

From now on—and far, far into the foreseeable future—teachers and other educators will be spending a good part of their out-of-school lives struggling with the *what* of the Common Core State Standards. Inevitably, outside experts will be hired to provide thousands of hours of in-school workshops and seminars, as well as off-site events that will be designed to help teachers learn how to change their practice to implement CCSS. But all this professional development will not help teachers figure out how to embed CCSS into their practice—and professional development will certainly not focus on how teacher collaboration can play a central role in teachers' learning *how to teach* to those standards.

Here's something to think about. While the focus of CCSS is on teachers' *teaching* and students' *learning,* the Standards for Professional Learning—developed by Learning Forward with contributions from 40 professional associations and education organizations—are focused on teachers' *learning.* Learning Forward's widely accepted multilevel set of standards

> outline the characteristics of professional learning that lead to effective teaching practices, supportive leadership, and improved student results. The Standards [for Professional Learning] make it explicit that the purpose of professional learning is for educators to develop the knowledge, skills, practices, and dispositions they need to help students perform at higher levels.[5]

The standards call for "professional development that fosters *collective responsibility* for improved student performance."

The Standards for Professional Learning reflect the latest research on effective teacher performance and recognize that teacher *collaboration* can have a profound effect on student performance. The standards essentially state that teachers, working together, will learn what they need to learn to improve teaching and assist all students in meeting challenging state academic achievement standards.

This does not guarantee that all teachers will be equally effective, but it does create an intellectually stimulating climate and a process through which educators' collaborative learning and mutual accountability can focus on improved student performance. This will enable educators to consider learning as an integral part of their workweek, and the standards posit that teacher learning "must be as easily accessible in their schools as walking to a room down the hall."[6]

Not by coincidence, but by design, Rounds is perfectly positioned to give teachers the tools, skills, strategies, and supports they will need to align their practice with the Standards for Professional Learning and thus open the door to the world of CCSS.

Alignment of Teacher Rounds to Standards for Professional Learning[a]	
Standard	*Connection to Rounds*
Learning Communities Core elements: • Engage in continuous improvement • Develop collective responsibility • Create alignment and accountability	• Commits to collective improvement through observations, feedback, and targeted action. • Focuses on "our" students instead of "my" students. • Adjusts and improves practice, holding all participants accountable for their work.
Leadership Core elements: • Develop capacity for learning and leading • Advocate for professional learning • Create supporting systems and structures	• Builds capacity of teachers to serve as facilitators. • Defines the role of facilitator; requires the skills of a teacher leader. • Develops a culture in which teachers are willing to make their practice public and transparent. • Creates collaborative structures for work with peers to support mutual learning.

(Continued)

(Continued)

Standard	Connection to Rounds

Resources
Core elements:
  • Prioritize human, fiscal, material, technology, and time resources
  • Monitor resources
  • Coordinate resources
	• Uses internal resources by developing teachers to learn with and from one another.
	• Experiments with and monitors new teaching strategies in classroom teaching.
	• Achieves the highest levels of return for teachers and students through a low-cost, high-impact professional development initiative.

Data
Core elements:
  • Analyze student, educator, technology, and time resources
  • Assess progress
  • Evaluate professional learning
	• Gives teachers opportunities to collect data from students and peers during an observation.
	• Develops teachers' capacity to assess instruction and analyze results.
	• Evaluates professional learning by using records of practice as a focus tool for teacher learning.
	• Uses data from student and teacher classroom practice.

Learning Designs
Core elements:
  • Apply learning research, theories, and models
  • Select learning designs
  • Promote active engagement
	• Provides job-embedded collaborative learning opportunities.
	• Encourages teachers to voice their concerns about their teaching; teachers are receptive to learning from one another.
	• Offers group-developed online resources in Google Docs; includes videos and records of practice.
	• Delivers facilitator coaching.
	• Specifies professional reading.

Implementation
Core elements:
  • Apply change research
  • Sustain implementation
  • Provide constructive feedback
	• Applies change research; teachers create an action plan, take action in their classrooms, refine action based on feedback.
	• Provides ongoing professional learning for teachers regardless of years in the field; recognizes the centrality of continuous improvement for all teachers.
	• Extends, refines, and sustains learning through specific feedback.

Outcomes
Core elements:
  • Meet performance standards
  • Address learning outcomes
  • Build coherence
	• Aligns with CCSS as well as any school or district initiative; can be focused on implementation of the initiative.
	• Reinforces teachers' observation and analysis skills; coordinates these to adjust practice and assess growth.
	• Links professional learning to student learning with a focus on student content standards.

[a]Adapted from Learning Forward's Standards Summary: Standards for Professional Learning. Retrieved from http://learningforward.org/standards-for-professional-learning#.UfkwsFOGH.

3

Who Does Rounds?

The Rounds Group

Once a Rounds group gets its rhythm and members begin to see the value of their collaborative efforts, it is important to be open and honest about the instructional practices that make a difference in student learning. If teachers develop practices that promote student learning but they keep the strategies to themselves, distrust and bad feelings can result if the "covert operation" becomes public.

Challenges for the Group

- Not having a shared language to talk about teaching and learning
- Not having the same kinds of expectations for teaching practice
- Understanding how best to follow through with individuals
- Keeping the focus on the work—without overgeneralizing or theorizing
- Working on practice, with emphasis on instruction

The guiding principle of a Rounds group should be this: All adults are committed to the success of all other adults.

The Rounds Facilitator

A Rounds group is a team, and all teams need leadership to be success-ful. The team leader in Rounds groups is the facilitator. The facilitator might be a designated teacher leader or be chosen by her or his col-leagues or the principal. She or he is responsible for establishing and maintaining an environment in which members feel safe having their practice observed, taking risks, and contributing to group discussions and processes to improve their practice and advance their learning.

The facilitator both models and teaches the different protocols and gives members confidence in the process—taking responsibility for the agenda and timing, and subtly guiding and redirecting the conversation when needed.

Promoting a shared vision of teaching and learning, the facilitator is a resource for suggestions, support, and follow-up conversations about pedagogy, continually reinforcing the guiding principle that Rounds is about changing practice, not just talking about practice. The facilitator is an active, careful listener, helping unpack teachers' underlying assumptions about teaching and learning so as to deepen the conversation and complicate teachers' thinking—helping them connect their observations and changes in their practice with effects on student learning. The facilitator affirms teachers and their work, as well as holding them accountable, individually and to one another.

Teachers are generally accustomed to preparing and teaching on their own, which is why learning how to observe and wonder in col-laboration with other teachers is a learned skill that takes continued practice. It takes awhile for teachers to understand connections between their different observations and wonderings, and to see pat-terns. This nonjudgmental process can be frustrating to those who want immediate solutions to their problems of practice. Only through the iterative process of Rounds can teachers gain clarity and develop hypotheses about how to improve their teaching and student learning.

It is quite natural, as they embark on the journey of Rounds, for teachers to feel insecure and defensive even as they are highly invested in and committed to the process. Teachers may have mis-guided assumptions about the purpose of Rounds, believing that the process will be used by supervisors for evaluative purposes. Both the facilitator and participants must be careful about any conversations they have with a supervisor that would serve to undermine the trust that allows risk taking.

Facilitators have the difficult and complex role of guiding in subtle, affirming, and flexible ways. To think about and deepen the conversation, the facilitator must be mindful of facilitation dilemmas such as these:

Challenges for Facilitators

- Understanding the data—What's relevant to observing practice, and what's not? How do we limit less relevant observations?
- Recognizing and interpreting different observations—When the observation looks for the wrong thing, how do we respond?
- Determining how to keep the focus on analysis rather than advice
- Knowing when to push—and how hard
- Gaining a sense of what it looks like to develop an area of practice over a long period of time
- Having confidence in one's own practice—not looking for approval from the group (For example, it is not unusual for the facilitator, acting as the first host teacher, to get the most negative feedback. There is no facilitator present to act as a guardian of the conversation.)

Facilitator Study Groups

Schools are discovering the value of having facilitators meet in monthly study groups to give them the opportunity to share with colleagues their dilemmas of practice, increase their expertise, and support one another as they learn the core skills of facilitation. If you're interested in thinking about focusing on increased student learning in your study group, use the video case in Chapter 6 (V6.1—Examining One Teacher's Change of Practice). Case studies with discussion questions are provided in Chapter 7. An essential question for facilitators: How can we nurture the capacity for rigorous and respectful critique?

The Host Teacher

Preparation for the Observation

The facilitator helps host teachers prepare for their observations and coaches them through the process, modeling respect and care for each person in the group, a desire to learn and grow, and openness to feedback and suggestions.

It is easy to assume that Rounds observation is simply an activity in which teachers observe a teacher teaching a regular class, take notes, and give feedback. The process is much more difficult and complex than that, requiring deep reflection and preparation on the part of the host teacher. Host teachers and Rounds groups often find that preparing for that role is the part of the hosting process that is critical to the success of the observation, and to the success of the Rounds group in learning from the experience. Needless to say, rigorous preparation is vital for success.

Before Rounds members observe a class, the host teacher needs to become clear on how the problem of practice is to be the focus and be able to describe specifically how it presents itself in the particular class he or she wants the teachers to observe. The host teacher should choose a class in which the problem is evident and a "problem," rather than a class that the teacher feels is going well.

With the facilitator's assistance, the host teacher fills out the Host Teacher Preparation Form (Figure 3.1) and distributes it to Rounds members, along with the date, time, and room of observation. The host has to make sure there are chairs and adequate space in the classroom for the observers.

The host teacher has had to think ahead about the particular lesson and articulate the lesson objectives and the specific lesson plan (subject to some change, based on what happens in class in the intervening time). The host then needs to be able to envision moves that both he or she and students are likely to make during class. What does the problem of practice look like? What is the task? What is the teacher saying? What are the students doing? What would the teacher like the students to be doing? The teacher needs to understand what is happening now in the class before any interventions can be made to change the practice. The host teacher writes specific directions for what and how teachers should observe that will provide useful data relating to the problem of practice. The host also determines to what degree (if at all) the observers may interact with the students.

The facilitator helps the teacher become clear about the problem of practice, hone in specifically on all elements of the instructional core, and understand what is happening now in the class before he or she can make the interventions necessary to change practice. Important learnings can sometimes depend on bringing the host teacher to an uncomfortable place of disequilibrium—any change can be daunting, and changes in a teacher's practice especially so. Here is the place for the facilitator to be the teacher's cheerleader and champion supporter as the teacher prepares to invite a group of peers to observe his or her class.

Figure 3.1   Host Teacher Preparation Form

To help focus the Round, please fill out this form and e-mail to your Rounds group.

Name _____   **Date of Round** _____

1. **Review/explain problem of practice.**

2. **Provide context for the lesson.**
   - What is the task?

   - What is your role as the teacher?

   - What are the students going to be doing?

3. **On what should the observers focus their attention?**

4. **To what extent should/would you like observers to interact with students?**

Following the Observation

At the Rounds debrief meeting following the observation, the host teacher briefly summarizes the problem of practice so as to focus the teachers' observations and wonderings. The host's role is then to listen quietly and take notes, if desired. At the end of the process, the host will have a chance to offer his or her own wonderings and learnings about the class, and to respond to teachers' observations and wonderings.

Following the meeting, the host teacher has the opportunity to debrief with the facilitator and articulate what he or she learned from the preparation for hosting, the hosting, and the Rounds debrief.

NOTE: Refer to Chapter 5, "How to Implement Rounds," to find all the tools and protocols necessary for preparing the host teacher.

PART II

Facilitators

4

How to Prepare
for Rounds

We hope the preceding chapters have given you enough of an in-depth background and introduction to the *what*, *why*, and *who* of Rounds that you are now well prepared to go on to tackling the next steps necessary to become a full-fledged facilitator. Yes, it is now time to roll up your sleeves and apply that accumulated knowledge to the work of learning *how* to actually *prepare for* and then *implement* Rounds for teachers.

Step 1: Lay the Groundwork for Collaboration

Establish Norms

Making progress in building an effective Rounds group is more easily accomplished when group members don't get stuck in unproductive patterns of behavior (agenda items pile up; some agenda items always get pushed aside; some people don't contribute while others do the work; productivity is low; ad inf.).

The solution is to develop and institute agreed-upon meeting norms that include a clear set of rules and processes as well as give minority voices confidence that they will be heard. Norms are behavioral guidelines that signify ways of being together and learning from one another. They help participants think about how to treat one another's ideas and how to push their own thinking.

An Example of Group Norms

Communication

- Listen—without interrupting.
- Stay focused and avoid tangents.
- Ask questions.
- Use humor.
- In group conversations, make "pass" an option.
- Limit distractions.

    o No cell phones
    o No sidebar conversations
    o No classwork

- Be aware of your "air time."
- Keep discussions confidential.

Relationship

- Support active/full participation by all members.
- Assume good intentions.
- Don't shoot down others' ideas.
- Embrace mistakes as opportunities.

This is, however, just one example. Each group needs to discuss and decide for itself what its operating norms ought to be—with the understanding that this is not a permanent document. It can change and be revised as different issues surface. Another perspective on norms:

- We will encourage asking challenging questions.
- We will take risks, value mistakes, and learn from them.
- We will check for understanding.
- We will encourage full participation.

Learn How to Observe: Conduct a Rounds Observation Workshop

Observation is a challenging skill and, like other skills, must be learned and practiced to achieve proficiency. Because of the cultural norms of teacher privacy, and the vulnerability teachers experience when they open up their classrooms to colleagues, it is important to practice the skill of observation before you begin to do a Round.

This almost goes without saying, but it's important to keep in mind that facilitators, too, need a good grounding in the skills of observation before they can hope to be effective in their role. For facilitators as well as teachers, learning to observe Rounds is like

Figure 4.1   The Rounds Process

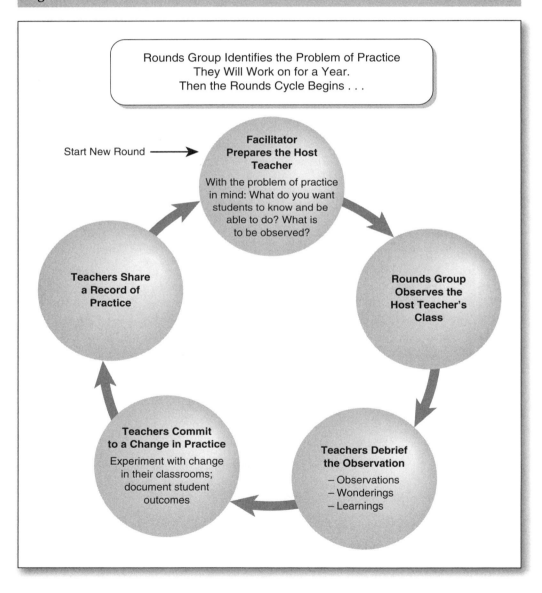

studying a new curriculum before you teach it. Study the observation workshop materials well, and get your head around the protocols before presenting them to your Rounds group.

It will be useful for all members of your group to start with a fresh introduction to the kind of Rounds practice we present in this facilitator's guide (see Figure 4.1). It makes good sense, therefore, to begin Rounds in your school with a 1-hour Rounds Observation Workshop, an introduction to and instruction in the special demands placed on teachers engaged in this rigorous process. Remember:

> The beginning is the most important
> part of the work.

> —Plato

To learn more about how to conduct an Observation Workshop, see Appendix D.

Step 2: Conduct the Introduction to Rounds Meeting and Choose a Problem of Practice

This is the most important instruction you will read here: *Your thorough preparation prior to each Round is absolutely critical for achieving success.*

Facilitator: Consider the annotated "Agenda for Meeting Introducing Rounds" a lesson plan, and prepare accordingly. Gather the materials necessary and allocate enough time for the meeting. Prior to the meeting, make enough copies of all the materials for all participants and put them into a Rounds folder for each group member. This will serve as a collection of documents and materials as your group becomes more robust.

- Agenda for Meeting Introducing Rounds (Figure 4.2)
- The Instructional Core (Figure 4.3)
- Choosing a Compelling Problem of Practice (Figure 4.4)
- Sample Problems of Practice (Figure 4.5)
- Ground Rules for Observing Rounds (Figure 4.6)
- Rounds Observation Worksheet (Figure 4.7)
- First Rounds Debriefing Protocol (Figure 4.8)
- Records of Practice for Rounds (Figure 4.9)

Figure 4.2   Agenda for Meeting Introducing Rounds

Time allocation: 1 ½ hours

Outcomes:

- Address the question: Why do Rounds?
- Begin to develop a culture of shared inquiry and collaboration.
- Begin to understand the role Rounds can play in sustaining ongoing teacher learning.
- Introduce protocols.
- Understand the roles and expectations for participants.
- Choose a problem of practice.
- Build community.

1. Purpose of Rounds

2. How We Will Work Together: Overview

3. Choosing a Compelling Problem of Practice

The facilitator's job is to make sure the problem of practice is an appropriate one. It should be

a. high-leverage aspect of teaching, where small changes in teacher practice will yield significant improvements in learning;

b. actionable—something teachers can do to change, in small increments;

c. relevant to all parts of the instructional core (Figure 4.3)—the relationship of students and teachers in the presence of content. Anything you do that does not result in an observable effect on this relationship is wasted time and resources.[a] In other words, a problem of practice that does not address improvements in teaching practice, the type of content given to students, and the role students play in their own learning will not affect the instructional core and is therefore ineffective in helping the group reach its goals.

4. Using Protocols

5. Next Steps/Meeting Times

[a]City, E. A., Elmore, R. F., Fiarman, S. E., & Teitel, L. (2009). *Instructional rounds in education: A network approach to improving teaching and learning.* Cambridge, MA: Harvard Education Press.

Agenda for Meeting Introducing Rounds (Annotated for the Facilitator)

Time allocation: 1 ½ hours

1. Purpose of Rounds

Facilitator's preparation: Read Chapter 2: Why Do Rounds? In addition, read the following and put in your own words.

Introduce Rounds with an explanation that includes these points:

- The goal is professional learning—with the ultimate goal of improving student learning.
- Rounds develops teachers' teaching capacity, mentoring/coaching capacity.
- Stress that Rounds is not evaluative.[1] There is a goal of learning together and continuing to reflect on what we're doing, modifying as necessary.
- Emphasize that the purpose of Rounds is not to have open-ended discussions about teaching and learning, or a way to feel better about our work life or our teaching. Focus on experimenting with new strategies, with the goal of enhancing our repertoire and improving student learning.

2. How We Will Work Together: Overview

NOTE: This is just an outline; we'll return to the details of each aspect later in this chapter.

Based on a problem of practice that we'll choose to work on together . . .

- During the year, each teacher will have the opportunity to **host a Round,** to be **observed** by everyone in the group. Based on our problem of practice, the host teacher will tell the group what the specific problem of practice is—based on what we'll decide during this meeting—explain what he or she wants us to observe, and provide the general context of the class. (The specifics of this will be explained using the Host Teacher Preparation Form.)
- Everyone in the group will **observe and take notes** on their Observation Worksheet. (Some schools may provide an alternative of

---

[1]Teachers may have misguided assumptions about the purpose of Rounds, believing that the process will be used by supervisors for evaluative purposes. Both the facilitator and participants must be careful about any conversations they have with a supervisor that would serve to undermine the trust that allows risk taking.

videoing for those teachers who are unable to come to the Round; however, nothing replaces a live observation.) Emphasize the ultimate goal—everyone should observe everyone.

- At the following session, the Rounds group will **debrief the observation** using a protocol.
- Each group member will **commit** to apply something he or she has learned from this observation to his or her own practice. Part of this commitment will include a **record of practice** so that the teacher can measure what he or she is changing and how it impacts student learning. As you introduce this aspect, be sure to emphasize that this is an important aspect of Rounds that should not be omitted, but assure participants that you will explain details later.
- During the next group meeting, each of us will **share a record of practice** from our own improvement process.
- At the end of each session, we will **reflect** on the session: what went well, what we learned, what we might want to change.

3. Choosing a Compelling Problem of Practice

The work of Rounds is collective. It is true that the work of teaching demands an individual capacity for spontaneity, improvisation, and good judgment, but it is also true that what our colleagues do matters as much to our students' learning as what we do. Therefore, the problems of practice need to be mutual ones. The following activity is so important because we may fail to see our individual problems of practice unless we inquire about them together.

Videos: Choosing a Compelling Problem of Practice

V4.1 Choosing a Compelling Problem of Practice—High School (5 mins.)

This group of six high school teachers are piloting a Faculty Rounds group, with support from the administration. In this video, they use the "Stones in Our Shoes" activity to begin developing their problem of practice.

V4.2 Choosing a Compelling Problem of Practice—Elementary School (8 ½ mins.)

A 3rd- and 4th-grade Rounds group (four teachers and two student interns) in an urban elementary school meet to develop a problem of practice. An interesting conversation emerges about benefits and challenges of focusing on writing, and the purposes of writing.

The facilitator's job is to make sure the problem of practice[1] is an appropriate one. It should be

a. a high-leverage aspect of teaching, where small changes in teacher practice will yield significant improvements in learning;
b. actionable—something teachers can do to change, in small increments;
c. relevant to all parts of the instructional core (Figure 4.3)—the relationship of students and teachers in the presence of content. Anything you do that does not result in an observable effect on this relationship is wasted time and resources.[2] In other words, a problem of practice that does not address improvements in teaching practice, the type of content given to students, and the role students play in their own learning will not affect the instructional core and is therefore ineffective in helping the group reach its goals.

Figure 4.3   The Instructional Core[b]

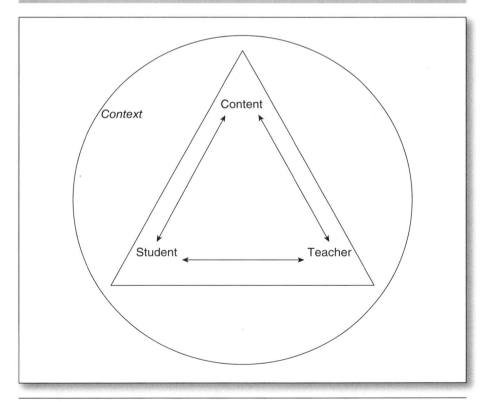

[b]City, E. A., Elmore, R. F., Fiarman, S. E., & Teitel, L. (2009). *Instructional rounds in education: A network approach to improving teaching and learning.* Cambridge, MA: Harvard Education Press.

Facilitators: It may seem like a trifle, but make sure the teachers in your Rounds group focus on these points during a Rounds meeting when you are discussing your group's problem of practice. These points are extremely critical, and it is our experience that it can be difficult for all participants to focus collaboratively.

A highly effective way to find a problem of practice is for the facilitator to lead a collaborative process where those involved in Rounds choose an appropriate problem of practice in which all have a shared interest—one that is *compelling*. You can start with the worksheet Choosing a Compelling Problem of Practice (Figure 4.4).

Figure 4.4   Choosing a Compelling Problem of Practice

Stones in Our Shoes

[T]he stones in our shoes—we like to feel them down there working things out—those little homes.

—Adam Chiles, "All Day in Shoes"

The stones in our shoes are the things that nag at the edge of our consciousness, the small irritants that demand just a bit of our attention every day, whether we want to give it or not. But those stones can also be "little homes" for the questions or concerns that can lead us to identifying meaningful problems of practice.

Brainstorm a list of the things that you wonder about in your classroom, beginning with questions, worries, and issues you haven't been able to "work out" yet. Write down at least five topics, and don't censor your list.

Five "Wonderings" or Stones in My Shoes

1.

2.

3.

4.

5.

Be specific in your concerns.

Why do I think this topic will sustain my interest?

Four examples of compelling problems of practice can be seen in Figure 4.5. (For an example of a problem of practice aligned to the Common Core State Standards, see Appendix E.)

Ideally, the Rounds facilitator can move teachers away from items that do not meet these requirements and in the process begin to help teachers become more aware of these criteria as a focus for changing their practice. But the main advantage of a facilitated, collaborative process is that it has teacher buy-in. There is a deeper understanding of the problem of practice when teachers have discussed it in depth before choosing it, and the choice of a problem of practice begins to form the trust that will be a foundation of the Rounds work.

Where do facilitators get the ideas for a problem of practice, and what do they do if no one in the group, including the facilitator, really understands what will make a good problem? In such cases, it may make sense to look at areas of core teaching practices that could serve

Figure 4.5 Sample Problems of Practice

Group A
Teachers have not provided enough targeted, consistent instructional opportunities for students to write authentically about their reading in both informal and formal reading tasks.

How do we use whole-group and small-group instruction to provide consistent instructional opportunities to write about reading?

- *Explain and expand in writing the deep conversations students have with each other.*
- *Write in order to support high-level comprehension.*
- *Express feelings that a book evokes in writing.*
- *Reason in writing.*
- *Cite evidence from text.*
- *Expand on ideas.*
- *Structure written responses to reading.*

Group B
Group work in our school is ineffective; sometimes only a few students do all the work, and that allows free rides for many students. Students resist helping other students succeed.

How can teachers make group work more effective in terms of student responsibility for their own and others' learning?

- *What tasks are appropriate for group work?*
- *How can teachers help develop the social and emotional skills needed for group work?*

(Continued)

Figure 4.5 (Continued)

- *How are the products of group work used in the context of a unit?*
- *How can teachers establish routines and habits needed for student focus and accountability?*
- *How do we assess group work, and what do we assess (product, process, both)?*

Group C
Students are not given opportunities to engage in critical thinking and problem solving with other students to help make the subject matter meaningful.[c]
How do we

- *encourage all students to ask critical questions and consider diverse perspectives about subject matter?*
- *help students analyze and draw valid conclusions about content being learned?*
- *provide opportunities for students to think, discuss, interact, reflect, and evaluate content?*
- *provide opportunities for students to learn and practice skills in meaningful contexts?*

Group D
Differentiation is challenging for our teachers.

How can teachers engage and support all students in learning?

- *How can teachers support students at different levels in a class through activities and questioning strategies to develop skills in understanding key concepts and issues and to initiate their own problem inquiry and solving?*
- *How can teachers use a variety of instructional strategies and resources that respond to students' diverse needs?*
- *How do teachers assess (during the course of class) the effectiveness of their different instructional strategies (i.e., the desired outcomes of the student engagement)?*

[c]Adapted from the New Teacher Center Professional Teaching Standards Formative Assessment System (1997).

as prompts to develop the problem of practice. Many of these practices are embedded in the standards espoused by the Common Core State Standards:

A. Schoolwide Expectations of Good Teaching

One such example may be schoolwide emphases on specific core teaching practices. Examine closely what your school thinks are critical areas of investigation—for example, how to make collaborative learning productive for all students, or how to cover the curriculum while employing collaborative learning, or how to hold students individually accountable for learning in collaborative groups, and so on.

Another resource for ideas for problems of practice is the Common Core State Standards. The task is to take a standard, narrow it down to one or two elements that constitute the standard, and figure out a question of teaching practice related to that element of the standard as the problem of practice.

B. *Common Questions That May Help Identify Problems of Practice*

- Are students engaged in high-level or low-level tasks? Do teachers ask high-level or low-level questions?
- Do teachers do most of the talking and thinking in the classroom?
- Are students able to articulate their thinking in writing?
- Are students able to transfer learning from one content area or grade level to another?
- Is students' understanding in mathematics conceptual or only procedural?
- Are students active or passive participants in class?
- Are some students, such as those with special needs, English language learners, boys, or girls, performing as well as they might? If not, what does this look like in the classroom?
- Do teachers enact a high-level curriculum in a low-level way?
- How do teachers know what students know?
- How do students know the quality of their work?
- What role do students play in assessment?
- How do students talk with one another about classwork?
- How do we enable students of all abilities to engage in high-level (vs. low-level) tasks?

No doubt there are numerous concerns about picking a problem of practice off the shelf. It has to be an authentic problem of practice for the teachers in the Rounds group, since the Rounds observations and debriefings are more about learning from observing than learning from being observed—and the key point is that what one observes must apply to one's own teaching practice. And the problem of practice will require significant discussion so it is genuinely understood before being adopted. Sometimes teachers suggest it would be better for each to have her or his own problem of practice. But if we are committed to improving teaching and learning in the group, it is important to remember that coherence occurs when adults agree on what they are trying to accomplish and are consistent from classroom to classroom.

4. Using Protocols

It is important for you, the facilitator, to explain the importance of using protocols for this work. There may be strong opposition to the idea of protocols—viewed as an unwarranted interference in ordinary business. If the norms of private practice are alive and well in your school and teachers are used to ignoring the impact of practice on student learning, you may find there is a great deal of resistance to using protocols. When encouraged to try them anyway, even reluctant participants may find them useful, a way to break through unproductive habits of working together. Using protocols allows Rounds to become a more powerful opportunity for professional educators to take charge of their own learning. They can direct their Rounds toward managing the real problems of their own work, and toward meeting their students' real needs. Rounds builds on teachers' own intimate knowledge of their practice.

Share the following protocols that will be used during the observation and subsequent Rounds meetings: the Ground Rules for Observing Rounds (Figure 4.6), the Rounds Observation Worksheet (Figure 4.7), the First Rounds Debriefing Protocol (Figure 4.8), and the Records of Practice for Rounds (Figure 4.9).

5. Next Steps/Meeting Times

It is beneficial to have the facilitator be the first host teacher for an observation (revisit "A Rounds Group in Action" in Chapter 1). That puts the facilitator in the risk-taking position and also serves as a model

Figure 4.6   Ground Rules for Observing Rounds

- Observers are silent during the lesson; no side conversations.
- Observers remain in the classroom during the entire lesson.
- Observers will circulate freely when students are working individually or in groups, and move to the side or back of the room during whole-class discussions.
- Observers are encouraged to ask students questions about lesson when appropriate, with permission of host teacher. They refrain from teaching or assisting students.
- Observers make notes on individual student comments and conversations, noting the names of students, if possible. They may also use a seating chart to map student responses.
- Observers record examples of how students construct their understanding through the discussion and activities.

Figure 4.7   Rounds Observation Worksheet

Teacher _____   Date _____

Problem of Practice _____

Teacher actions, quotes	Student names, actions, quotes	Questions/analyses

Figure 4.8   First Rounds Debriefing Protocol

(1 hr., 15 mins.)

1. Sharing Observations

  a. Host teacher reflects on the lesson, explains what his or her goals were for addressing the problem of practice and in what ways goals were or were not met, and shares data on what students learned. (2 mins.)

  b. All observers take a few minutes to review notes and jot down specifics on the lesson, focusing on how the lesson attempted to address the problem of practice. (2 mins.)

  c. Observers share data from observation. What did you **see**? Use ***descriptive data*** only, not inferences or judgments. (10 mins.)

2. Wonderings/Open, Honest Questions

  What do you genuinely wonder about in what you saw in observation? These are open, honest questions. The questions should not have preambles, they should not be disguised advice, and you should not have a particular answer in mind. The point is not to offer solutions but to stimulate thinking. (10 mins.)

3. Selective Response by Host Teacher

  Respond to what seems most relevant to the problem of practice, extend a wondering, and so on. (3 mins.)

4. Learnings

  Each person will describe something he or she has learned from the observation and debrief. (10 mins.)

5. Commitments

  How will you modify your instruction based on what was learned during the observation and debrief? (15 mins.)

6. Developing a Plan to Experiment

  Teachers develop a plan to experiment with modifying their practice prior to the next Round: What commitment did you make, how did you implement it, what were the results? (5 mins.)

for other teachers when they complete their Host Teacher Preparation Forms and assume the role of the host in the debrief meeting.

The facilitator may want to say that she or he will be the first to be observed: "We'll practice on me. Here are the specifics: [date/time]."

It would also be a good idea to give out a schedule for the Rounds meetings for the rest of the year. The specific classroom observations need to be scheduled from month to month. Make sure to remind people how to observe the class.

Figure 4.9   Records of Practice for Rounds

Keeping track is a matter of reflective review and summarizing, in which there is both discrimination and record of the significant features of a developing experience. . . . It is the heart of intellectual organization and of the disciplined mind.

—John Dewey, *Experience and Education*

Records of practice—A record of practice is an artifact; it is something tangible from the realm of practice that can be studied by participants in the Rounds group.

We use artifacts to provide concrete evidence of changes made in teaching practice and student learning. This isn't about tracking progress but, rather, about tracking the *process* of changing our practice. When deciding on an artifact type, first consider the purpose of collecting the record of practice and the question of practice you have in mind. Then you can determine the artifact that best fits that purpose and question.

Examples:

- Lesson plan
- Discussion prompts
- Assessment
- Student work
- Teacher's journal
- Smart Board notes
- Video

The facilitator should complete the Host Teacher Preparation Form and e-mail it to the group.

Soon after the group has done its first observation is a good time to have a meeting to debrief the observation.

5

How to
Implement Rounds

Figure 5.1   The Rounds Process

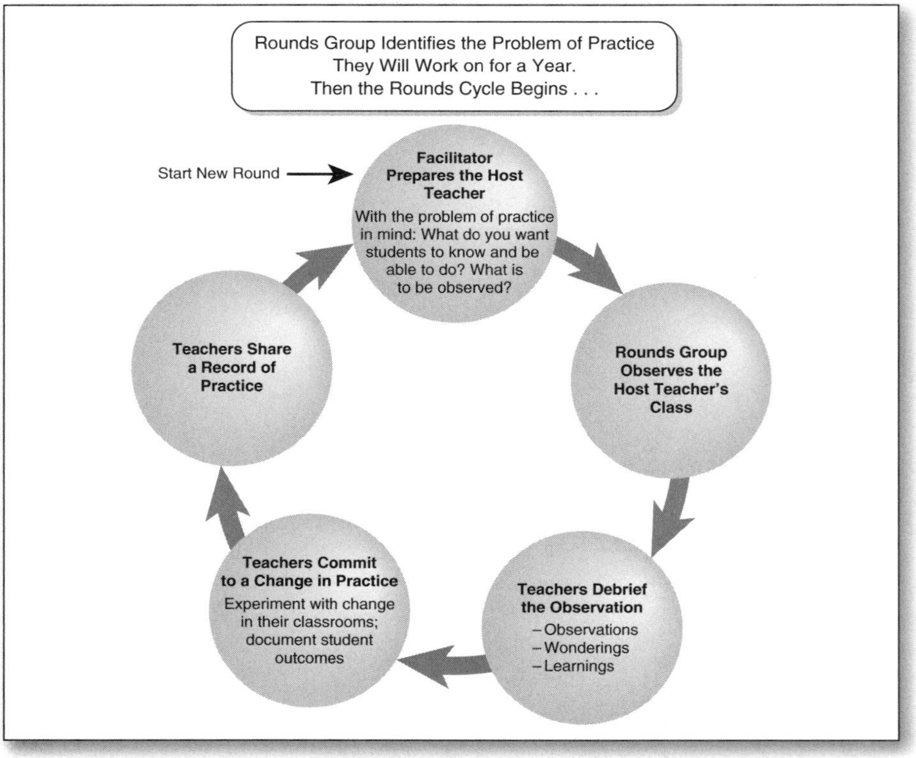

Rounds Group Identifies the Problem of Practice
They Will Work on for a Year.
Then the Rounds Cycle Begins . . .

Start New Round →

**Facilitator
Prepares the Host
Teacher**

With the problem of practice
in mind: What do you want
students to know and be
able to do? What is
to be observed?

**Teachers Share
a Record of
Practice**

**Rounds Group
Observes the
Host Teacher's
Class**

**Teachers Commit
to a Change in Practice**

Experiment with change
in their classrooms;
document student
outcomes

**Teachers Debrief
the Observation**

– Observations
– Wonderings
– Learnings

Step 1: Facilitator Prepares the Host Teacher

Facilitator: Consider the following a lesson plan, and prepare accordingly. Gather the materials necessary and allocate enough time for the meeting. Prior to the meeting, study the Host Teacher Preparation Form and the Facilitator's Protocol for Preparing the Host Teacher below.

● ●

Facilitator's Protocol for Preparing the Host Teacher

Time allocation: 45 minutes to 1 hour

Facilitator's Preparation

- Review the Host Teacher Preparation Form (Figure 5.2).
- Read the descriptions below.
- View a Host Teacher Preparation video (Video V5.1 and/or V5.2 for high school, and/or V5.3 for elementary school).

● ●

Supporting the Host Teacher in Preparing the Form

The Host Teacher Preparation Form is a vital component of the Rounds process. It is an opportunity for you and the host teacher to review together the problem of practice and develop a plan for how the lesson to be taught will attempt to address that problem. It also is a chance to focus the observers by specifying the kind of data the host is interested in collecting.

As the facilitator, you play an important role in coaching the host teacher to complete the Host Teacher Preparation Form. A possible cycle: Meet with the host teacher to determine the class to be observed and how to complete the form. After this meeting, ask the host to complete a draft of the form and e-mail it to you.

If necessary, meet with the host again, ask the host to revise the form, and have the host send the form to the group at least 3 days before the observation is scheduled.

Figure 5.2   Host Teacher Preparation Form

To help focus the Round, please fill out this form and e-mail to your Rounds group.

Name _____   **Date of Round** _____

1. **Review/explain problem of practice.**

2. **Provide context for the lesson.**

   o   What is the task?

   o   What is your role as the teacher?

   o   What are the students going to be doing?

3. **On what should the observers focus their attention?**

4. **To what extent should/would you like observers to interact with students?**

Using the Host Teacher Preparation Form

1. Review the problem of practice.

Help the host clarify his or her own specific problem of practice that is connected to the broader problem of practice the Rounds group has agreed to address. It is important for the host to choose a class where that problem is evident. Since teaching has traditionally been a private practice, it goes against the culture of teaching to choose a class that is not going smoothly. It is important to emphasize this counterintuitive move from the beginning. The purpose of Rounds is *not* a dog and pony show but, rather, a place where teachers build trust in one another to enable the risk-taking experience of being observed teaching a challenging class.

2. Provide context for the lesson.

- What is the task?

    Remind the host teacher to focus on clarifying the task. It is the task that predicts performance. The real accountability system is in the tasks students are asked to do.
- What is your role as the teacher?
- What are the students going to be doing?

    Be sure to have the host teacher explain how the lesson fits into the broader unit and how this lesson attempts to address the problem of practice. Any new strategies the teacher will use during this lesson to address the problem of practice should be highlighted. Make sure that the host teacher answers the three questions above (parts of the instructional core).

3. Give specific directions for how observers should observe.

This may seem very straightforward, but, in fact, this is an opportunity for you to give some very specific teaching. In this section, the host may want to jump ahead to solve the problem. Your role as the facilitator might be to slow down the conversation, to help the teacher unpack assumptions about the students, the content, the school culture, and so on. You may want to ask the teacher to explain what is happening now and his or her "vision of the possible."

4. To what extent would you like observers to interact with students?

Encourage the host teacher to allow observers to talk with students during independent or group work. Interesting questions to ask a student might be, "Why do you think your teacher asked you to do this work?" or "How is the work you're doing connected to the goal of the lesson?" or "What's hard for you in this lesson?"

After the host teacher e-mails you the first draft of the Host Teacher Preparation Form, you have a good opportunity to make comments and suggestions on the form to clarify every section. Often these sections are hard to complete—each has its challenges for the novice host teacher. (See an example of a Host Teacher Preparation Form with the facilitator's comments in Figure 5.3, and analyze the comments you find there.)

Figure 5.3   Host Teacher Preparation Form With Facilitator's Comments

Note: Underlined comments are the facilitator's tracked changes sent to the host teacher.

Rounds: Host Teacher Preparation Form

To help focus the round, please fill out this form and e-mail to your Rounds group.

Name _____   **Date of Round** _____11/15/2012_____

1. Review/explain problem of practice.

The problem with which I am concerned is motivation. How do we motivate our students, especially those who don't want to be in class? In particular, how do we motivate seniors, who have already "checked out"? Additionally, even if we cannot motivate some students, how do we deal with their presence in class? How do we make sure that their lack of motivation doesn't spread and "infect" other students?

Is there a way to bring this back to the group's problem of practice?

Remember the problem of practice: Teachers aren't fostering high-level discussions with students who have limited content knowledge. We will increase the level of thinking and discussion by asking students to *support their comments* with textual evidence and respond to each other, not repeat one another, to ask clarifying questions of one another, to be specific about what they agree with and what they disagree with, etc.

I wonder if you could engage students by becoming more of a facilitator during discussions—more student centered.

Perhaps it would help for you to review the instructional core—to improve practice, the teacher, content, and student all need to be affected by the change. Though it's true you can only change yourself, the teacher needs to change the **role** of the student in the lesson—partner learning, students taking some kind of leadership role in the discussion. If the expectations for the role of the student don't change, the intervention won't be successful. AND we all know blaming the students doesn't work.

2. Provide context for the lesson.

The class I am teaching on Monday is about the Nazi conquest and racial reorganization of Poland after September 1, 1939. This class will be the first one after our seminar, in which the students (without me) discussed and determined whether the Germans as a people invited, allowed, and embraced the Nazis as their totalitarian government. Before the seminar, we examined the rise of the Nazis into power and then the construction of the Nazi totalitarian state. The class, as a whole, has been an investigation of the Holocaust as a prime example of 20th century genocide. Major questions we are examining include the following: How does genocide happen? What steps need to be taken before a genocide can occur? Who is culpable for genocide?

o   What is the task?

The class that I teach is composed of 20 students of all different ability and performance levels. In general, the girls are more active participants and score higher on assessments. While most of the students are engaged in the class, there are a few who are clearly "clocking time." These individuals rarely, if ever, prepare for class, rarely, if ever, prepare for the reading quizzes, and rarely hand in reading responses.

It would be great if you could describe what you expect students will know and be able to do as a result of this class.

o   What is your role as teacher?

I plan to have a discussion based on the major questions mentioned above. I will highlight the important points that emerge from the discussion and put them on the Smart Board.

o   What are the students going to be doing?

Participating in the discussion and taking notes on the main points.

3. On what should the observers focus their attention?

I have a few concerns that I feel are somewhat related to the issue of motivation:

1. Some students say very little, if anything, while others tend to dominate the discussion.

    a. The students who say very little in class discussion either sit inert or periodically engage in side conversations.

2. Some number of students come to class unprepared, and even the threat of reading quizzes doesn't seem to faze them.

3. Some students have a habit of showing up late to class, and the loss of participation points (application grade) doesn't seem to deter them.

4. Despite being seniors (or maybe because of being seniors) some students in the course cannot help but interrupt other students. Admittedly, this concern doesn't have so much to do with motivation, but I wanted to put it in anyway because I find it a real challenge.

5. How do I deal with "smart-ass" comments from a particular student, which seem to come from two places (I think): (a) a belief in his inherent comedic skill and (b) a desire to cover up the reality that he hasn't actually prepared for the class.

Knowing that these issues exist, what are you going to do to try to change this up? You don't need other teachers to affirm that this is really going on. We've all had experience with this. But, thinking about the instructional core, what interventions might you make to address one or more of these issues?

(Continued)

Figure 5.3 (Continued)

Maybe you would like teachers to record the kinds of questions you ask or keep track of the verbal flow in the class or something about how time is divided in the classroom, or the flow of the class and the modalities you use and if there's a relationship between student participation and how you set up the discussion.

4. To what extent should/would you like observers to interact with students?

During discussion involving the whole class, I would prefer that the observers not interact with the students. Please feel free to examine their texts, notice any side conversations or irrelevant writing (laundry lists, notes to significant others, forged permission slips, etc.), but try to avoid distracting them. Also, please do not participate in the discussion. I will ask the students to do a little group work, and when they are in groups, please feel free to circulate and listen to different pairs, making notes of things you see and hear that are relevant to our focus on the dynamics of discussion with an emphasis on student-centered conversation. However, try to avoid asking them about the content of the class.

What is your worry about doing this—there's so much to learn from talking to students.

Don't Forget the Kids

Maybe you teach in a school where students are accustomed to having groups come into their classroom from time to time and they're comfortable with that. Maybe not. In any case, students should be made aware of why people are in the room observing them.

Students might assume that the group is there to see how well they behave and follow directions. As a result, they might clam up or wait for the visitors to leave before they risk saying something "wrong." On the other hand, if students know the observers are there to see the kinds of questions students ask, they might be more inclined to ask them.

When a Rounds group comes to visit, students might be distracted wondering why teachers whom they know but who don't generally come into their class are there.

Give your host teacher a little coaching about how to make students a part of the conversation about Rounds. Rather than feeling like lab animals in an experiment, they should feel empowered to know ahead of time that their teacher is still learning and trying to improve his or her practice.

A favorite anecdote of ours: During the second year of Rounds in a local high school, students asked during the first few days of school, "What's your problem of practice this year? Last year we really helped Mr. [Smith] when we found out he was supposed to ask us to do more of the thinking in class. We worked on asking good questions and challenging other kids in the class during discussions. Don't worry; we'll get you a good grade."

Videos: Preparing the Host Teacher

 V5.1 Host Teacher Preparation—High School 1 (7 mins.)

The Rounds group facilitator meets with the host teacher to help him prepare the Host Teacher Preparation Form. Note the questions she asks to make sure that the form is clear and that the participants know specifics of what to observe.

 V5.2 Host Teacher Preparation—High School 2 (5 mins.)

The facilitator helps the host teacher prepare his Host Teacher Preparation Form. Note how the facilitator pushes the teacher to be specific about the kind of discussion he would like students to engage in during class. Without being specific about outcomes, it's difficult for the teacher to plan the lesson. The facilitator suggests class guidelines so students will be clear about the teacher's goals for a discussion. After spending a year in Rounds, the teacher wonders if "there's a possibility that [the discussions aren't] different but that I'm different."

 V5.3 Host Teacher Preparation—Elementary School (5 mins.)

The facilitator coaches a teacher brand new to the Rounds process in preparing her Host Teacher Preparation Form. Note the moves the facilitator makes to help the teacher focus on the problem of practice.

Step 2: Rounds Group Observes the Host Teacher's Class

Everything has been prepared. The Rounds group teachers have been thoroughly briefed on how to use their Observation Worksheets, they have studied the Host Teacher Preparation Form, and they are ready to use the observation protocols to which they have agreed.

Step 3: Teachers Meet to Debrief the Observation

Facilitator's preparation: Consider the following a lesson plan, and prepare accordingly. Gather the materials necessary and allocate enough time for the meeting. Prior to the meeting, review these materials:

- First Rounds Debriefing Protocol (Figure 5.4)
- Protocol for the First Debriefing Session—annotated (see below)
- Guidelines for Asking Honest, Open Questions (Figure 5.5)
- Records of Practice for Rounds (Figure 5.6)
- Rounds Debrief Meeting video (Video V5.4 or V5.5) to discover the moves the facilitator made

Make enough copies of Figures 5.4, 5.5, and 5.6 for all participants.

Videos: Rounds Debrief Meeting

 V5.4 Rounds Debrief Meeting—Elementary School 1 (10 mins.)

 V5.5 Rounds Debrief Meeting—Elementary School 2 (17 ½ mins.)

In each of these videos, teachers debrief a Rounds meeting. Notice how the debrief begins with honoring commitments. Think about the purpose of the wonderings. What can be gained by "wondering" about a practice rather than falling into the more commonplace habit of giving advice? Also notice the new commitments --do they build on previous commitments?

Protocol for the First Debriefing Session (Annotated for the Facilitator)

NOTE: Annotations are shown in italics.

Time allocation: 1 ½ hours

1. Sharing Observations

a. Host teacher reflects on the lesson, explains what his or her goals were for addressing the problem of practice, describes in

Figure 5.4   First Rounds Debriefing Protocol

(1 hr., 15 mins.)

1. **Sharing Observations**

   a. Host teacher reflects on the lesson, explains what his or her goals were for addressing the problem of practice and in what ways goals were or were not met, and shares data on what students learned. (2 mins.)

   b. All observers take a few minutes to review notes and jot down specifics on the lesson, focusing on how the lesson attempted to address the problem of practice. (2 mins.)

   c. Observers share data from observation. What did you **see**? Use ***descriptive data*** only, not inferences or judgments. (10 mins.)

2. **Wonderings/Open, Honest Questions**

   What do you genuinely wonder about in what you saw in observation? These are open, honest questions. The questions should not have preambles, they should not be disguised advice, and you should not have a particular answer in mind. The point is not to offer solutions but to stimulate thinking. (10 mins.)

3. **Selective Response by Host Teacher**

   Respond to what seems most relevant to the problem of practice, extend a wondering, and so on. (3 mins.)

4. **Learnings**

   Each person will describe something he or she has learned from the observation and debrief. (10 mins.)

5. **Commitments**

   How will you modify your instruction based on what was learned during the observation and debrief? (15 mins.)

7. **Develop a Plan to Experiment**

   Teachers develop a plan to experiment with modifying their practice prior to the next Round: What commitment did you make, how did you implement it, what were the results? (5 mins.)

what ways goals were or were not met, and shares data on what students learned. (2 mins.)

Teacher explains what his or her goals were for addressing the problem of practice, describes in what ways goals were or were not met, and shares data on what students learned.

Possible pitfalls:

- *Host teachers tend to over-explain and apologize for goals that weren't met during the lesson.*
- *Participants want to ask questions about decisions the teacher made during the lesson.*

Intervention:

- *Remind teachers that the debriefing protocol is tightly timed and that time set aside for commitments cannot be honored if the group gets bogged down here.*

b. All observers take a few minutes to review notes and jot down specifics on the lesson, focusing on how the lesson attempted to address the problem of practice. (2 mins.)

*Suggest to participants that they review their notes and highlight sections that address the host teacher's problem of practice and relate to Part 3 of the Host Teacher Preparation Form—**on what should the observers focus their attention**. Remind participants that they should focus on data only—no interpretations or analyses during this section—but they can note any questions or wonderings they may have and use those later in the debrief.*

c. Observers share data from observation. What did you **see**? *Use descriptive data only,* not inferences or judgments. (10 mins.)

- *The goal during this phase is to look at instruction in a way that helps participants understand what is really happening in the classroom. This involves collecting and citing evidence so all participants can come to a shared understanding of the facts. Acknowledge that when we observe instruction we want to draw inferences, but during this phase we want to suspend any judgment and simply describe what we see.*
- *Encourage descriptive language to bring out details of what was seen. Encourage participants to describe teaching and learning using evidence. You may also push people to connect their evidence to the focus of the observation. Sometimes people are so worried about making a judgment that they make descriptive comments that aren't relevant for the problem of practice (e.g., "All the students were using dictionaries").*
- *Suggest to the group that in the spirit of safety and trust, the first few comments could be "warm" observations.*

- *Promote respectful conversation, and be careful not to allow the conversation to become critical. Even in a data-driven conversation, participants can focus on students' not paying attention or question the teacher's choice to cold call even when that's not the problem of practice.*

2. Wonderings/Open, Honest Questions

What do you genuinely wonder about in what you saw in observation? These are open, honest questions; they should not have preambles, they should not be disguised advice, and you should not have a particular answer in mind. The point is not to offer solutions but to stimulate thinking. (10 mins.)

This is a complicated aspect of Rounds. Make sure participants don't use this part of the protocol to make comments in disguise. It takes a while to know how to state an open, honest, authentic wondering. For assistance with that, see Figure 5.5, Guidelines for Asking Honest, Open Questions.

Suggestions for facilitators to use during the "Wonderings" section of the debrief protocol follow:

- *Separate out informational questions.*
- *Facilitator can indicate that a wondering is clearly judgmental.*
- *Facilitator can model building on someone else's wondering.*
- *If a wondering is to blame the kids (e.g., "They aren't intellectual," "Too many SPED students," or "They don't want to do the work; they're seniors"), as the facilitator, you might reframe the comment and wonder, for example, "Is there a pedagogy that can help include more of our SPED students?" Put the onus on the teacher.*
- *If wonderings become repetitive, all proposing the same point of view, the facilitator might take on a different perspective to push participants' thinking.*

3. Selective Response by Host Teacher

Respond to what seems most relevant to the problem of practice, extend a wondering, and avoid questions he or she knows the answers to, as those are not generative for the host's learning. (3 mins.)

Possible pitfall:

- *Host teacher wants to respond to every wondering without attention to how well it connects to the problem of practice.*

Figure 5.5   Guidelines for Asking Honest, Open Questions

Adapted from Dr. Parker J. Palmer, The Center for Courage and Renewal.

"[I]n support of the rule 'no fixing, no saving, no advising, no setting each other straight' and in support of our intention to help each other listen for inner truth."[a]

1. **An honest, open question** is one that you cannot possibly ask while thinking, "I know the right answer to this."

   Example: "I wonder why you didn't have more structure in the lesson. Have you considered adding more structure in the lesson?" This question is not an honest question, because the asker assumes he or she already knows the answer.

   Better: "I wonder—what impact does the structure of the lesson have on student participation?"

2. An honest, open question **does not have an obvious answer.**

   Example: "Is this your normal routine?" This can be answered with a simple yes/no and thus does not generate much discussion or learning.

3. Ask questions that are **brief and to the point**. Don't lard them with rationales and background materials that allow you to insert your own opinions or justify your advice.

4. Ask questions **aimed at helping the focus person explore** his or her concern, rather than satisfying your own curiosity.

5. **If you aren't sure** about a particular question, sit with it for a while and wait for clarity.

Learning to ask honest, open questions is challenging. We may slip occasionally into old habits of trying to "fix" others. It helps to continually remind ourselves that our purpose in this exercise is not to show what good problem solvers *we* are but, rather, to support another person in listening to his or her own inner teacher.

[a]Parker, P. J. (2004). *A hidden wholeness: The journey toward an undivided life; Welcoming the soul and weaving community in a wounded world.* San Francisco: Jossey-Bass. (Quote on p. 114.)

Intervention:

- *You can refocus and remind the host teacher to select no more than two or three wonderings to respond to.*

4. Learnings

Each person will describe something he or she has learned from the observation and debrief. (10 mins.)

During this round of the discussion, invite participants to share what they will take away from observing the class and the subsequent conversation, something they personally learned. Teachers could also comment on aspects of the discussion that helped them realize something that's important to them in their practice.

5. Commitments

How will you modify your instruction based on what was learned during the observation and debrief? (15 mins.)

Everything you and your Rounds group have done up until now has been prologue. All the steps, all the work, all the time, discussions, effort, sweat, and tears have been preparation leading up to the main event — changing practice. The Rounds group has observed, wondered, and reflected on what they've learned.

Every step completed has been a de facto commitment to take teaching practice to the next level — to uncover more, learn more, do more. The whole purpose of Rounds is to lead to a change in teaching that will result in an improvement in practice and, ultimately, to an improvement of student learning.

Ask participants to make a commitment to change their instruction.

In many schools, the protocol breaks down here, at the stage of committing to changing practice. It is particularly important that you and the teachers in your Rounds group understand the importance of this step.

When teachers make commitments, ask them, "How will you measure what you've committed to, and how will you report on it in the next Round?"

6. Develop a Plan to Experiment

Teachers develop a plan to experiment with modifying their practice prior to the next Round. Be prepared to share at the next Round: What commitment did you make, how did you implement it, and what were the results?

Be sure to record the learnings and commitments the participants make and send it to the group shortly after the Round. It is also helpful to resend this 1 week prior to the next Round, as a reminder to bring a record of practice.

Provide your group members with the Records of Practice for Rounds handout (Figure 5.6), and spend time modeling your example of a record of practice.

Figure 5.6   Records of Practice for Rounds

Keeping track is a matter of reflective review and summarizing, in which there is both discrimination and record of the significant features of a developing experience. . . . It is the heart of intellectual organization and of the disciplined mind.

—John Dewey, *Experience and Education*

Records of practice—A record of practice is an artifact; it is something tangible from the realm of practice that can be studied by participants in the Rounds group.

We use artifacts to provide concrete evidence of changes made in teaching practice and student learning. This isn't about tracking progress but, rather, about tracking the *process* of changing our practice. When deciding on an artifact type, first consider the purpose of collecting the record of practice and the question of practice you have in mind. Then you can determine the artifact that best fits that purpose and question.

Examples:

- Lesson plan
- Discussion prompts
- Assessment
- Student work
- Teacher's journal
- Smart Board notes
- Video

Step 4: Group Conducts the Next Rounds Meeting

Your next Rounds meeting will begin with the subject of honoring commitments: What have you done since the last Round? What evidence (record of practice) have you brought? And then, you start all over again, from Step 1. Another host teacher is selected, another class is observed, you have a debriefing, you commit to a change of practice based on the observation and debriefing, and you share a record of practice.

However, notice in the Rounds Debriefing Protocol (Figure 5.7) that one component (Number 1: Honoring Commitments) has been added to the protocol that you used for your first meeting. This is the protocol you will use for all subsequent Rounds debriefings.

During this Round, you will begin by asking teachers to report on what they've tried in their classroom since the last Round (when they made a commitment) and this Round. All the records of practice should have been posted on the school's shared website (e.g., Google Docs) before this meeting. Encourage the sharing of an artifact using the Records of Practice handout (Figure 5.6) as a guide. Teachers are in general not prepared to share records of practice in this way, and it will take time for them to develop the habit of documenting their commitments. You may want to choose only one or two teachers each month to explain their artifacts in more detail. It is important for you to have a well-developed artifact to model the process.

Developing a List of Common Criteria

About four times a year, pause after the "Honoring Commitments" section and work on developing a list of criteria that address the problem of practice. The criteria should be teaching strategies teachers would agree they want to see in a classroom. The question they're addressing is, "What would it look like if we were successful in solving this problem of practice?"

Step 5: Teachers Share a Record of Practice

Examples of Commitments to Change and Records of Practice

(As reported by teachers during a Rounds debrief)

Example 1

Step 1: Commitment

One teacher's commitment: "In my freshman class where the participation is not what I would like, I will call on every student in the class—cold calling. I will inform the students that I am planning to do this to increase their role in the class and that every student will speak at least once during the class discussion. I will track the comments they make and whether students are raising their hands more often as a result of this intervention."

Step 2: Record of Practice

Next month, the teacher reported, "Everyone gets called on every day in the class. This intervention totally has changed the

Figure 5.7   Rounds Debriefing Protocol

(1 hr., 15 mins.)

1. **Honoring Commitments**

   Review briefly what you have done since the previous month's meeting, and share records of practice showing evidence of that commitment. (15 mins.)

2. **Sharing Observations**

   a. Host teacher reflects on the lesson, explains what his or her goals were for addressing the problem of practice and in what ways goals were or were not met, and shares data on what students learned. (2 mins.)

   b. All observers take a few minutes to review notes and jot down specifics on the lesson, focusing on how the lesson attempted to address the problem of practice. (2 mins.)

   c. Observers share data from observation. What did you **see**? Use *descriptive data* only, not inferences or judgments. (10 mins.)

3. **Wonderings/Open, Honest Questions**

   What do you genuinely wonder about in what you saw in observation? These are open, honest questions. The questions should not have preambles, they should not be disguised advice, and you should not have a particular answer in mind. The point is not to offer solutions but to stimulate thinking. (10 mins.)

4. **Selective Response by Host Teacher**

   Respond to what seems most relevant to the problem of practice, extend a wondering, and so on. (3 mins.)

5. **Learnings**

   Each person will describe something he or she has learned from the observation and debrief. (10 mins.)

6. **Commitments**

   How will you modify your instruction based on what was learned during the observation and debrief? (10 mins.)

7. **Develop a Plan to Experiment**

   Teachers develop a plan to experiment with modifying their practice prior to the next Round. (10 mins.)

dynamic in my class. Students can't just zone out. And for some students they have become more participatory. Students who never raised their hand now raise their hand. I told the kids I was going to do this during every class and they said okay. No problems with kids adjusting to it. I was worried they wouldn't think it was fair or would be embarrassed. Next year I will try this in the beginning of the year to get more people participating. It can change the culture of my class. Students expect that I will lecture if they don't participate. Now they understand that I expect them to do the intellectual work."

Example 2

Step 1: Commitment

The teacher: "I will create the space and opportunity to help kids do the work so that I don't do the work for them. I want to find the right amount of scaffolding they need to do the work. I will think of setting it up and giving them enough time—I will make a video as my record of practice."

Step 2: Record of Practice

"The first piece of scaffolding I provided was to break down the key pieces of the assigned text so that each one would mean something different."

The teacher then showed her video (her record of practice) and asked the following questions of the Rounds group:

1. Did my scaffolding steal away some of the intellectual work? Did I overstep?

2. Do you think breaking down the verse into three pieces was helpful?

Rounds participants wondered whether the teacher should have allowed the students to complete the worksheet on their own first, without so much explanation.

The teacher wondered, when she realized the students were stuck in a way she hadn't anticipated, what kinds of questions she could have asked to help them be more successful.

"I thought the way I had organized the materials would yield something new and worthwhile. I thought filling in the worksheet was easy, but even the filling in was more challenging than I thought."

Step 3: Refining the Commitment

During the next Rounds meeting, the teacher said, "I will continue trying to step back and be more conscious about giving students the space. I will continue to video my class because, more often than not, when I video it makes me more aware when I don't shut up when I should. I'm more thoughtful in advance—this is an area that kids will need more room. At this point 60% of the time my misguided instincts kick in—I can explain this better than anyone here, so I start. That deprives the students of doing the critical thinking work. I'll bring in another clip next time."

Yes, It *Is* a Circular Path to Perfection

You and your Rounds group have now completed all the steps illustrated in Figure 5.1, The Rounds Process. You have

- identified a problem of practice,
- prepared the host teacher,
- observed a host teacher's class,
- debriefed the observation,
- committed to a change of practice,
- shared a record of practice, and
- continued the process.

All successful schools—whether charter, traditional, or independent—have features in common: a clear mission, talented and dedicated teachers, time for teachers to work together, and feedback cycles that lead to continuing improvements. What Rounds provides is a platform for talented teachers to work together, with an expectation that built-in feedback cycles will lead to continued improvement.

6

Year-End Wrap-Up

Has the Work Improved Student Learning?

Okay, Rounds group facilitator, it's coming to the end of the year. You and your group have worked really hard. You've taken all the lessons provided in this book to heart, and now you want to know if your group actually accomplished its goals. That's why a year-end wrap-up is so important.

Obviously, you are keeping this thought uppermost in your mind: *Has the work we have tried so hard to do all year really improved student learning?* That's a simple and yet very complicated question. It's tempting to suggest that almost anything you do will improve student learning, but you know from experience that there is the real possibility that not everything you do in the classroom translates directly into measurably positive outcomes.

As you review your group's progress over the year, you may be asking a couple of big-picture questions:

1. How can we measure the effectiveness of professional learning?

2. Is there a time frame within which you can expect professional learning to improve student learning?

Unfortunately, for a lot of professional learning initiatives, the only evaluation has been the traditional end-of-program "smiley" sheet on which participants report their degree of "satisfaction" with the program, presenter, and facilities. Rarely, if ever, does the evaluation sheet even mention anticipated outcomes.

Some argue that it is impossible to link professional learning with student achievement because of the large number of intervening variables. Yes, there are many variables that are difficult to assess, but you will be better able to understand those variables because your Rounds group has gone through these three important phases:

Phase 1: Using their problem of practice, teachers in a Rounds group develop a list of features (common criteria) of practice that teachers agree they want to see in a classroom and that they can then use to analyze their practice.

Therefore, after each Rounds debrief, the criteria are reviewed and additional criteria may be added. At the end of the year, each Rounds group is expected to produce a list of criteria that can be shared with the entire faculty. The goal is to develop an increasingly more refined vision and articulation of what good teaching at your school would look like.

Phase 2: These criteria are then used as indicators that the teachers' practices are moving in the right direction. Teachers develop a vision of what good practice looks like in a classroom when teachers use these criteria in a robust way.

Phase 3: The records of practice serve as a ground plan, based on the criteria developed during Phase 1. At the conclusion of Phase 3, each teacher, working with a partner, prepares a presentation for the Rounds group that includes student work to show improvement in student learning. They understand (from the Common Core State Standards) that the success of any curriculum must be demonstrated by the quality of student work—that is, for students to be able to apply their learning, autonomously and thoughtfully, to varied complex situations.

All that may be theoretical, but luckily we have documented proof that Rounds—in real-life situations—really does accomplish what we say it will. That brings us to the video of a year-end Rounds group, and the answer to our question: Has our work led to an improvement in student learning?

The Answer Is Yes!

Video Case: Examining One Teacher's Change of Practice

Video V6.1 uses an excerpt from an end-of-year Rounds group meeting to show how teachers use the Rounds group and records of practice to study and question their practice to improve their students' learning opportunities.

In the video, you'll see a math teacher share her artifacts with the Rounds group, explain the changes she made in her practice, and describe the effect of her innovation on student learning.

The video is instructive for two reasons: It demonstrates how one teacher used the process of Rounds to change her practice (i.e., Rounds actually works the way it's supposed to), and it shows how a Rounds meeting can be organized to present records of practice.

Framing the Context

The teachers in this high school Rounds group chose their problem of practice: **How can teachers facilitate learning experiences that promote autonomy, interaction, choice, and responsibility?** (Some schools phrase their problems of practice as "questions of practice.") Over the course of a school year, the teachers met monthly; each hosted at least one classroom observation, and at the last meeting of the year all the teachers presented the results of their work with records of practice. This video highlights the presentation made by Alexandra ("Alex") of her artifacts—her accounting of her record of practice, slides of the development of her goals over the year, samples of her students' written critique of her change of practice, and her own assessment of how successful she feels in having met her goals.

There are three options for using this video case:

- Facilitators can use it with their facilitator study group.
- Facilitators can use it with their Rounds group to give teachers a model of an end-of-year Rounds group meeting.
- Facilitators can use it for viewing by themselves to see a model of an end-of-year meeting, including assignments and moves made by the facilitator.

Before watching the video clip, read and review the following (10–15 minutes):

1. Spend a few minutes digesting the details of the assignment that the facilitator sent to the Rounds group (Figure 6.1) a month before the final meeting of the school year.

2. Examine the artifacts that Alex provided:
   - Summary of Alex's record of practice (Figure 6.2)
   - Alex's Host Teacher Preparation Form (Appendix F—Optional)
   - Alex's Student Slides (Appendix G)
   - Student feedback e-mails (Appendix H)

Figure 6.1 Facilitator's Assignment to the Group

To make sure that each teacher's presentation represented his or her year's work and that the range of the group's accomplishments was highlighted at the meeting, the facilitator sent all the group members the following e-mail:

Dear Rounds Group,

I'd like to use our last Rounds meeting of the year to analyze the records of practice you developed throughout the year. Please bring to the meeting evidence (a record of practice) of a <u>change in your teaching practice</u> from this year, based on our common problem of practice. What does the innovation look like when it is in use? What would we observe teachers and students doing in a classroom that is using this innovation well?

As you prepare for your presentation, review the <u>common criteria</u> we developed that indicate our practice is moving in the right direction, and ensure that students can apply their learning without significant scaffolding by the teacher:

<u>Students</u>

- Students talk to one another, challenging one another's ideas.
- Students reference one another's ideas.
- Students are focused on task, cross-checking, probing.
- Students take initiative to check their work (rather than have to be told to).
- More knowledgeable student in a group helps a student who doesn't understand by guiding him or her, rather than just giving the answer.

<u>Teacher</u>

- Asks really good questions that are focused on problems rather than telling what he or she wants students to know
- Doesn't answer his or her own questions
- Uses wait time
- Doesn't answer student questions—directs them back to students
- Asks higher level questions on Bloom's Taxonomy (e.g., apply what you learn to something new)
- Provides opportunities for students to work independently or in groups

Remember that your evidence of change in practice could be

- Discussion: Questions I ask, how students respond, to whom they respond, when they challenge one another, and so on.
- Student assignments: How does the assignment support students doing the intellectual work? More opportunities for students to do critical thinking.
- Assessment of student work: Analyze assessments from teachers that indicate how students are doing the intellectual work.

Before our meeting, meet for an hour with a colleague from our group to refine your record of practice that reflects a change in practice. With your partner, reflect on the following:

- *Which criteria have the teacher worked on, and how?*
- *What was the task in which this artifact was created?*
- *How does the artifact relate to the problem of practice?*
- *How does the artifact represent progress in teaching practice and student learning? Examples of student work.*
- *Using the agreed-upon criteria, what is different in your practice now as a result of the work you have done on this problem of practice?*

I look forward to our meeting. Thanks.

In the video, you'll notice that Alex presents both the slides that she uses with students and her student e-mail responses as artifacts for part of her records of practice presentation. This directly correlates to the Common Core State Standards having to do with connecting students to the work of the Common Core. Educators can and should talk about the Common Core standards with their students. Connecting what high school students say they need with the standards that guide instructional decisions can help students achieve post-secondary success.

Video: Sharing Records of Practice

V6.1 Examining One Teacher's Change of Practice (10 mins.)

Alex, a 10th-grade math teacher, shares her records of practice in a year-end wrap-up meeting with her Rounds group, connecting her classwork with the Common Core State Standards.

View the video and respond to the following questions:

1. What is the goal of the year's final Rounds group meeting?

2. How does Alex describe her intervention to support students' math understanding?

3. In what ways does Alex say the Rounds group influenced her practice?

4. Given the lack of consensus in the e-mails from the students, what would you suggest Alex do next year?

Figure 6.2   Alex Summarizes Her Record of Practice

Following receipt of the facilitator's assignment, Alex sent her e-mail to teachers in the group describing how she responded to her problem of practice. Note how she reviews her problem of practice, comments on what she will show the group at their meeting, and makes plans for how she will use this professional development tool in the coming year.

Dear Friends,

My question of practice focused on my 10th-grade Advanced Algebra 2 classes and a problem that they were having when it came to retaining concept knowledge and maintaining skills related to previously learned material. Based on the Wonderings and Learnings you so thoughtfully presented at my feedback session, I decided to institute a routine with two new aspects: (1) a first slide of the day on my Smart Board that included the goals of the day in a mix of student-friendly and academic language, and (2) a second slide either immediately following the first or later in the period that had one to three "warm-up questions." These questions varied in form between individual and group work, skills-based versus concept-based, and "math" work versus writing about math.

The goals for my record of practice were to (1) frame the lesson, (2) improve retention of content knowledge, and (3) establish a formal, daily routine for the class. Feedback from students was positive throughout. Students actually complained when the warm-ups were not there. Warm-ups were always visual (written and shown on the Smart Board) and orally presented by me to accommodate multiple learning styles. I also always went over the goals and warm-ups with students.

Included in my record of practice are three slides—one developed early in the year before I started improving my goals slide, and two examples of goals and warm-up slides after my Rounds team visit and feedback session. I also will present e-mails from four students responding to questions about the success of my implemented routine. I sent surveys to a sampling of all the students in the class, and four of them responded. One of the four had begun the year with an F and worked his way to an A by the end of the year.

I see the routine as a success, as I know (from examining the students' math notebooks) that students used the warm-ups to track their own progress and they used the goals to review what they had learned before assessments. I plan to continue and expand this innovation. I may ask students to offer warm-up questions ahead of time and/or ask students to read ahead and write goals for the lessons. However, I will keep a teacher-generated approach at least half of the time so as to provide direction, guidance, and a model.

Regards,

Alex

5. How did Alex's partner help her with the preparation of her records of practice presentation?

6. What could Alex have done to make her presentation stronger?

The Power of Teacher Rounds

The video and its accompanying artifacts help demonstrate that Rounds is not only doable, it also values the intellectual work of teachers and provides a form of group professional learning that does not involve the addition of an outside consultant. In Rounds, teachers work on problems that are focused on improving student learning, thereby increasing the chances that the changes developed through Rounds will actually be implemented by members of the group. Not only can Rounds improve the work of all the teachers in the group, it can deepen their thinking about curriculum and instruction, and sharpen teachers' intellectual growth and power.

End-of-Year Reflections

We hope you will use the instructional power of video to record some of your Rounds meetings and analyze them throughout the year—at least one or two, and especially the wrap-up meeting at the end of the year. It's also helpful to reflect on the year gone by, and the group-participation questionnaire in Figure 6.3 could serve to guide you through the process.

Figure 6.3   End-of-Year Rounds Reflections

I. I used to think that Rounds would be . . .

    Now I think . . .

2. If you had known in the beginning of the year what you know now about Rounds, what would you have done differently?

3. In what way did you grow your teaching practice this year? What is your evidence of improvement?

4. What changed for you as a collegial coach during Rounds' discussions?

5. In what specific way(s) would you like to grow your teaching practice next year?

6. The Rounds group has spent a year on its problem of practice _____ and has developed a set of common criteria* and behaviors. Please examine them and then refine and prioritize the list. The goal is to create a document that colleagues in other groups can use to analyze the school's teaching. These criteria can be used as indicators that we are moving toward improved teaching practice.

* Using their problem of practice, teachers in a Rounds group develop a list of features (common criteria) of practice that teachers would agree they want to see in a classroom. After each Rounds debrief, the criteria are reviewed and additional criteria may be added. Each Rounds group is expected to produce a list of criteria at the end of the year that can be shared with the entire faculty. Ultimately, the goal is to develop an increasingly more refined vision and articulation of what good teaching at the school would look like.

7

Cases and Guides to Case Analysis

Using Cases to Facilitate Discussion of Issues Confronting Rounds Groups

The use of teaching cases—also known as case studies—has played an important role in the education of physicians, attorneys, and business people for several decades. The power of cases is that they present and illuminate issues from the real world; they don't solve them. Instead, the study of a case facilitates an inquiry-based process that leads to discovery, understanding, and action.

Lately, schools of education and other venues of teacher learning have been applying this tool as a way to connect theory and practice, using it to examine problems of teaching practice.

> Cases . . . present ambiguous situations in which protagonists face difficult questions. A good case teacher [facilitator] aims to shape a discussion in which there is a high quality of analysis—not a single right answer.[1]

And here we would reiterate the phrase *not a single right answer.* There is no simple solution to any of the cases in this book—that's what can make them so powerful. Thus, the accompanying guides to analysis provide the necessary scaffolding for digging deeply into each Rounds case to uncover the layers of complexity and refine the interactions between teachers and facilitators. Our experience has shown us that excellent case facilitation can lead teachers to truly in-depth thinking and can result in the likelihood of positive long-term changes in practice.

How and When to Use Cases

Ideally

In some schools there is a monthly facilitator study group. We have found that time for facilitators to work together is one of the most important resources to improve facilitation practice. These case studies provide the opportunity for facilitators to tackle problems together, listen to other points of view, and share experiences from their own facilitation.

Alternatively

A. Use case studies with your Rounds group.

Providing your Rounds group with real-life dilemmas can test their thinking, challenging teachers to devise their own solutions. Cases are empowering, allowing teachers to engage in constructing their own professional development.

B. Use case studies on your own.

Analyzing these cases can provide a rich basis for developing problem-solving and decision-making skills. Analyzing each case and thinking about the questions can demonstrate both the problems and the possibilities of Rounds groups.

CASE 1

Choosing a Problem of Practice

How Do You Say, "The Fault, Dear Teacher . . ." While Avoiding the Blame Game?

It is the first meeting of the Teacher Rounds group at William Garrett High School, an urban school in the Midwest. Henry Arroyos, the principal, became interested in Rounds as a school improvement strategy and proposed that a Teacher Rounds project be initiated at Garrett High. Twenty-four teachers from several departments who teach different subjects and have different levels of experience volunteered to participate in the school's first three Rounds groups, each with a facilitator. One of those Rounds groups is now seated around a conference table. After a few minutes of getting settled in, they begin by following an agreed-upon protocol to consider what problem of practice they will be working on during the school year.

The group's facilitator is Carl Washington, an experienced, 9-year chemistry teacher and mentor, well liked and respected by both faculty and administration. He seemed to Principal Arroyos to be a natural choice for the role, and Carl accepted and participated in facilitation training over the summer.

"Okay, let's talk about how we should go about choosing our problem of practice," begins Carl. "This is new to all of us, so I think we should start by thinking about areas of our teaching that we want to improve on. Working on problems of practice is meant to be growth producing, not a way of evaluating. Each of us, myself included, has some aspects of our practice that we need to work on. To be a problem of practice for us to work on, it needs to involve all points of the instructional core—"

Carl refers to their handout, which is a diagram of the instructional core (see Figure 4.3 in Chapter 4).

"—meaning the teacher, the student, and the content. It also needs to be something we can observe directly, and something that is actionable—but not beyond our control—like the schedule, for example, that will make a difference in student learning.

"I want to point out an often used strategy of finding a problem of practice. It's tempting to think that all we have to do is look at the data—test scores are the most common example—and think to ourselves, 'Gee, that's easy. Problem solved. The test scores tell us everything we need to know!' But as a school we've decided that such an approach doesn't do anything to guide teachers toward strategies that help them change their practice. And that's the journey we're now embarking on . . . taking up the difficult challenge of changing our practice to improve student performance.

"I know you've given this some thought in preparation for today, so I'm going to have you take a few minutes more now to think quietly, using your 'Stones in Our Shoes' worksheet [see Figure 4.4 in Chapter 4], and write down those things that are on your minds that you would like to work on. Then we'll share our thoughts and ideas and strive to find something in common, as it will make our conversations more fruitful."

Shawn Ryan, a biology teacher in his early 40s who came to Garrett this year after experience as a mentor and teacher leader in another state, speaks first.

"Why do we have to find a common problem of practice?" asks Shawn. "Why not let everyone choose their own problem?"

Uh-oh, Carl thinks to himself. *How come he doesn't understand what we're doing here? This could be a long conversation, and I really don't want to spend time talking about this right now. It will distract us from our work.*

So he says, "Don't worry about that—as we work together and bring up our individual problems, I'm confident we'll find common ground and arrive at a problem of practice that works for all of us. We have to make sure that as we move along in this process we're all working toward common goals—even though, individually, we may take different approaches to solving our common problem of practice."

Shawn doesn't seem satisfied with this but decides not to respond except with a nod. The room is quiet for a few minutes while teachers write down their ideas.

Carl looks around, seeing everyone is done or has a lot on their page. "Are we ready to begin?"

Daniela Colombo, who teaches English, came to Garrett High 4 years ago after earning her master's in literature. She comments to Camilla, a second-year physics teacher sitting next to her, "I'm so excited we're going to be able to talk about our practice. We never have a chance to talk about what is really going on."

Carl: "Who'd like to start with something on their list?"

Alex Truffot, the music teacher, seems ready to offer a comment but stays silent.

Mary Harkin, a third-year history teacher, offers this: "The kids in my 10th-grade class like to discuss, and really get into it with each other. That's all good, but they come in hellbent on speculating and saying whatever they want, rather than backing up their ideas with evidence from their readings. They like to argue with one another but don't know how to prove their points. I love it that they are so involved, but don't know how to get them to also think."

Shawn: "Is it as big a problem in their *writing*?"

Mary: Oh, it's huge! They can't explain how they came up with an answer. I really notice it in their papers when they don't back things up."

Daniela: "Oh, yeah. Some kids are just not disciplined thinkers. Who's in your class? I bet I've taught some of those kids."

Carl tries to get the conversation back on track. "Let's not get into particular names. So let me see if I get this correctly—your problem of practice is how to help students develop their analytic skills, particularly in using evidence from the texts to develop their points. Is that right? You're trying to get them to use both their textbook and primary history texts?"

Mary responds, "Exactly. They totally forget about the primary texts, which I spend so much time teaching. How I can scaffold their skills in backing up their arguments both in discussions and in writing?"

"Great. Thank you, Mary."

Shawn joins in: "One problem I have is with the bio textbook. It won't allow me to do what I know is best for kids to help them learn. It's a problem because my department chair insists I use an inquiry-based learning approach to biology. I have trouble differentiating—some kids get it very quickly, and other kids not at all because they aren't patient enough with this approach."

Daniela: "Oh, I saw a great article about the pros and cons of inquiry-based learning. It says that—"

Carl thinks to himself, *Oh no, here comes a tangent that could go on and on.* With a smile, which he hopes doesn't look too forced, he interrupts Daniela and says, "Thanks, Daniela. Why don't you put it on our online conference?"

Shawn: "Another problem I have is that I talk too much in class."

Camilla Stanton asks, "Why do you feel that's a problem?" Camilla has been at the school for 9 years and teaches math. She is willing to try Rounds because she is frustrated that, no matter how hard she tries, many of her students don't improve.

Shawn responds, "Because then students don't model for each other, and I don't check for understanding."

Carl steers the conversation with, "You've brought up a few important problems of practice, Shawn—how to differentiate in a class with an inquiry-based approach, getting the students to do the learning from each other, and your checking for understanding."

Mary: "Yeah. That goes along with what I was saying. I guess I'm not sure my students really understand what I want them to do. They don't understand why they don't get A's on their papers, though I keep telling them they have to use evidence!"

Carl wonders to himself, *I think she's starting to think more about her problem, building on Shawn. Or is she just taking center stage?*

Daniela jumps in with, "The problem I'm really concerned about is, how do we motivate students, especially those who don't want to be in class? In particular, how do we motivate those seniors who have already checked out? Additionally, even if we can't motivate some students, how do we deal with their *presence* in class? How do we make sure that their lack of motivation doesn't spread and infect other students?"

Mary squirms a bit in her seat, then flashes an understanding smile and says, "Hasn't that happened to all of us!"

Camilla nods. "They're even worse before the holidays."

Shawn asks, "What have you tried, Daniela?"

Carl thinks, *I'd like to know the answer to that, too, but the first meeting on a problem of practice is not the time to be posing solutions.* He says nothing, though, hoping that Daniela will pick up on the cue to talk about the bigger problem that involves teaching practice.

"I try to give them multiple warnings," says Daniela. "But even the threat of reading quizzes doesn't seem to faze them. They rarely, if ever, prepare for class, rarely hand in reading responses. Even losing points off their grade when they come in late doesn't seem to deter them."

Carl offers, "That's certainly frustrating, and it is a problem, Daniela. I'm wondering if you can word your problem in language that talks about what *you* as the teacher want to do to improve the situation."

Carl hopes that he only imagines Daniela's smirk as she says, "How do I encourage seniors to stay motivated in class? How can I get them more involved and to make comments that are more appropriate? They make such smart-ass comments sometimes!"

Carl makes a note to himself: *She thinks it is all the kids' fault! How do I get her to question her own teaching—what she herself is doing—rather than blaming the kids? I'm afraid she could pull the whole group in that direction. How can I broach it with her without making her defensive? And what can I do in front of the whole group so we can end the meeting with one agreed-upon problem of practice?*

CASE 1 GUIDE TO ANALYSIS

Key concept: The facilitator's first job is getting the group to agree on what constitutes an appropriate problem of practice.

In this case, a Rounds group facilitator confronts the challenge of having teachers choose an appropriate problem of practice that is acceptable to them all. How can the facilitator direct the conversation toward an understanding that poor student performance is not necessarily the result of lazy or inattentive students but is connected to a problem of practice?

A. Analyzing the Case

Step 1: Read the Case (10 minutes)

Distribute copies of the teaching case and have the group read it through, underlining or highlighting pieces of information they think are significant to understanding the case.

Step 2: Establish the Facts of the Case (10 minutes)

As a whole group, make a list on chart paper of the significant "facts" of the teaching case. Include what you know about each team member. Try to withhold judgment, inferences, or evaluation, and come to agreement about what happened.

Step 3: Case Analysis Questions (10 minutes)

Discuss the following questions. For each question, identify the evidence that leads to your response.

1. What is this case about?

2. What key information do you have about the case?

3. What don't you know that you'd like to know?

4. What's the sticky issue in the case?

B. Planning Next Steps (20 minutes)

1. Review the case with a partner, and identify possible decision points in the case.

2. Are there any points during the Rounds meeting where Carl or another group member could have responded differently to have reached some common understanding of a generative problem of practice?

3. What advice would you give Carl? Would the instructional core diagram help him? Why or why not?

4. As a group, share some of your ideas.

Optional activity: **Role play** an interaction between Carl and Daniela after Daniela says, "How do I encourage seniors to stay motivated in class? How can I get them more involved and to make comments that are more appropriate? They make such smart-ass comments sometimes!"

CASE 2

Seeking Clarity of Instruction

Freedom Can Be Just Another Word
for Making Poor Choices

In an empty classroom at the Henry L. Belkin Middle School, Alicia, a veteran teacher leader and the Rounds group's facilitator, is helping Jason examine his upcoming role as host teacher. It is 2 weeks before he is scheduled to have teachers observe his class for Faculty Rounds. Jason, in his third year of teaching 8th-grade science, is anxious to develop possible ways he can address the Rounds group's problem of practice: *"How do I make concepts and skills clear and accessible to students?"* In addition, he is seeking guidance on how to fill out the Host Teacher Preparation Form.

Alicia has been looking forward to working with Jason because he likes to talk about his teaching and seems eager to try new things, many of which he has been learning from observing other teachers in Rounds.

This is Jason's first teaching job, and he has sought Alicia's advice on several occasions outside of regular group meetings. He has reported that his students don't seem to understand what the learning goals are for his lessons and that, at the end of each class, even though they have often learned a fair amount, they don't seem to realize what they have learned.

Alicia begins this meeting by asking, "Jason, what thoughts do you have about how you would like to work on 'clarity' during your host observation, and which class would be best for us to see in order to help you?"

"There are a lot of kids who are just so passive, particularly in my Period 4 class," says Jason. "I try to get them to answer questions, but they just sit there and stare at me, so I end up doing a lot of the talking. A lot of them aren't very strong in math. I'm thinking, if I could get them to participate more in class, they would get it better. So I wanted to try more group work. I will be sure to be clear in my directions. I will put them on the board. Then I will have a student read the directions out loud. I thought this would be a good thing for the Rounds group to observe, to see if asking them to do the intellectual work themselves, in groups, will help them be able to articulate what they've learned."

Alicia nods, but her mind is churning: *He is trying to solve their lack of participation, but he doesn't seem to be unpacking why they aren't participating. Clarity is way more than the directions for the assignment. Jason has mentioned several times that some of his students seem lost and have no idea how to do the problems he gives them. He's already told me about all the students he meets with for extra help. I need to help him get beyond thinking about them participating and start thinking about what he can do to make the material clear to them so they can participate.*

Alicia asks, "What do you want to have happen through the group work that isn't happening now with the whole class?"

"Well, if they do group work, they will have to do the thinking themselves, and then they will understand the material. In last month's Round, I saw the kids do group work in Monica's class, and they were so involved and engaged. I thought I would try her strategy."

"Okay," she says, "but what will you instruct students to do if they get stuck, or confused?"

"I'll have them ask their partner—or me. And they can use their book and their notes to refresh their memories."

Alicia ponders, *Is he unconsciously gravitating toward the group work that he saw Monica do because it's safer to try out something that's already been done, rather than wrestle with what he can do to make the concepts and skills he is teaching clearer?*

Out loud she asks, "So I'd like you to think about what you would like the teachers to observe in your class."

"Well," says Jason, "they can watch how students work in groups. Which kids dominate and which kids hardly talk? How are my group configurations working? What about the kid who has been absent recently—is he lost? There is one kid who always forgets his glasses— how is he doing? Which students are working hard? Who shows understanding and who doesn't?"

Alicia asks, "To do that, we'll need to know your objectives for the day. Can you explain exactly what the students will need to know and be able to do to solve these problems?"

"That's easy. Chapter 11, the problems at the end of the chapter."

"Could you be more specific?" replies Alicia. "What do the students need to know and be able to do in order to answer the problems?"

"That's all laid out in the book," responds Jason.

Alicia points out, "It will be important to make your objectives clear on your host preparation form so the teachers can look and see how the objectives are being met. It would also be a good idea to have us observe how you explain the objectives to the students." Jason nods and takes notes.

Alicia asks, "What would you like us to observe about your moves? In other words, what are *you* planning to do to make the material clear to the students?"

"I will just be circulating while they are doing the work. I'll be there if they need me."

Alicia prods further with, "What will you be doing when you are circulating around? If they say they are stuck, how are you planning to help them? Can you anticipate where they may need help so you can ask a question or give them a clue or scaffold the steps to help them get back on track?"

Jason mutters, "Okay, I'll think about that," looking away blankly.

Alicia is growing increasingly concerned. *He doesn't seem to understand the role he plays in student learning, group or otherwise. How is this observation going to improve his practice? What should I do? He seems pretty set on this group idea. But I don't think he gets it that the students won't be able to do the intellectual work until he makes the required knowledge and skills clear to them.*

"What instructions are you planning to give the students on how to do the work?" she asks. "Will you let them know what you expect of them in their group work, and what to do when they have questions?"

"All my classes are similar in structure. Because we have this pattern in class, they see how it works and what kinds of things I test and what I value. The kids know what I expect. But I will think about whether I should be more explicit with them."

Alicia points to her notebook and asks, "Would you like to take some notes to remind yourself of the questions you should be thinking about when you fill out the form?"

"Okay, good idea." Jason begins to write notes for himself, working on which students to put in which group.

Driving home that evening, Alicia cannot stop thinking about her problem as facilitator. *What chance is there that Jason will think more about my questions when he writes out his lesson plan and develops his host prep form? In the observation, will the group notice his lack of clarity and point that out to him? Should I have pushed him harder to directly tackle what I think is his real problem of practice? Would that be overstepping my bounds into a supervisory role, or is that necessary to make Rounds as effective as possible to improve teaching practice? How much freedom should a facilitator allow a host teacher in choosing how to address the problem of practice?*

CASE 2 GUIDE TO ANALYSIS

Key concept: The facilitator faces the problem of finding a balance between pushing a teacher toward addressing a real problem of practice and guiding that teacher toward self-discovery.

Jason, the host teacher for this month's Rounds group, has chosen to focus on how he does group work to increase student participation. Alicia, the facilitator, knows from observing previous classes that there is a far more pressing problem in Jason's teaching practice: His lessons lack clarity. To what extent should Alicia push Jason to tackle what she feels is his real problem of practice?

A. Analyzing the Case

Step 1: Read the Case (10 minutes)

Distribute the teaching case and have the group read it through, underlining or highlighting pieces of information they think are significant to understanding the case.

Step 2: Establish the Facts of the Case (10 minutes)

As a whole group, make a list on chart paper of the significant "facts" of the teaching case. Include what you know about each team member. Try to withhold judgment, inferences, or evaluation, and come to agreement about what happened.

Step 3: Case Analysis Questions (15 minutes)

Discuss the following questions:

1. How does the facilitator's role differ from the role of supervisor?

2. What is the facilitator's responsibility to the school to specifically address the problem of practice?

3. How do you create a Rounds culture that balances giving teachers voice and choice on the one hand and emphasizing accountability for student learning and academic achievement on the other?

4. What can Alicia do to support Jason while also pushing him to meet the demands of curriculum/standards/testing and accountability?

5. What are benefits and drawbacks of pushing a teacher to address a more challenging aspect of the problem of practice?

6. How does this discussion affect Jason? What are the feelings engendered for Jason around his conversation with Alicia?

B. Exploring the Dilemma of Balancing Inquiry and Advocacy

The facilitator's job is to promote an attitude of inquiry that leads to thoughtful problem solving among teachers. All too often, facilitators fall into the trap of advocating. After all, we have invested years gaining our knowledge, skills, and abilities, so shouldn't we be able to tell others what they need to do? Others err on the side of inquiry only. Who am I to tell you anything? Let's *reflect* together. Effective facilitators understand that a balance between inquiry and advocacy is critical. Facilitators are open to listening and know when to choose to advocate a position.

Consider these questions (10 minutes):

1. How does Alicia balance between inquiry and advocacy?

2. If you were Alicia's coach, how would you coach her?

CASE 3

Faster Isn't Necessarily Better

When a Principal Shortcuts the Rounds Process, What Gets Lost?

Yolanda Jones, 5th-grade teacher at the Gladwell Regis School, walks into Renee Williams's 1st-grade classroom. Renee, a widely respected teacher at Gladwell and a 6-year veteran, was named the teacher leader/teacher facilitator of the whole-school Rounds for Teachers groups by the school's principal, Claudia Garcia. At the beginning of the school year, Renee had been very excited about her new role.

It is now a sunny afternoon in late June, and Renee is cleaning out her room.

Yolanda is downhearted. "I'm sorry to have to say this, Renee, but not much has changed since we started this Rounds for Teachers stuff. The situation is kind of obvious. No one's going to use this idea next year. It takes too long, and there's not enough bang for your buck."

Renee is surprised, but she had already sensed that something wasn't working right with the Rounds group. Renee always pays attention to what Yolanda says, and now Yolanda's words make Renee doubly upset: *Is this how all the teachers feel? Has this Rounds idea been a total failure?*

The story of Rounds for Teachers at the Gladwell School all began after the principal, Claudia, sent Renee to a summer workshop on Rounds for Teachers.

Claudia had been the principal at Gladwell for 8 years and had regularly run the school's professional development, but over time she had become increasingly uneasy about her role.

"It's time for the teachers to take over their own PD," she had confided to Renee. "Teachers should take some leadership for what happens in their grade levels. I've been running things for too long. We need to see more teacher leadership here."

When Claudia found out about Rounds, a new PD tool for teachers, she believed she had found the answer to the teacher leadership problem.

"It looks like teachers run Rounds themselves," Claudia explained, when she approached Renee and asked her to take a summer workshop on Rounds to implement them at Gladwell.

Renee learned a great deal at the workshop and returned to the school reporting excitedly that Rounds works! "In Rounds, teachers develop a problem of practice under the guidance of a facilitator, prepare a lesson with a colleague using what they call a Host Teacher Preparation Form, present their problem using video, and then with the other teachers at the grade level, pursue answers to one important instructional problem, called a 'problem of practice.' Then they assess the results during regular Rounds meetings and hold each other accountable for making changes in their practice. You see, it's all connected to what is called the 'instructional core,' which is, in the simplest terms, the connection between the teacher and the student in the presence of content. And Rounds has been shown to improve student achievement. What could be better?"

Claudia ruminated a bit, read all the material Renee had brought back with her, and decided to take the plunge.

Why not? she thought. *I can't figure out how to hand over PD to the teachers, and this seems like a well-thought-out plan. It would force teachers to give each other the support they need, make their grade-level meetings come to life (beyond looking at the endless test score data we're handed), and might even get the school's standardized test scores to go up.*

So before the school year started, she and Renee discussed a strategy for implementing Rounds with all the school's grade-level teams.

However, to Claudia, the Rounds model that Renee presented to her didn't seem exactly right for the Gladwell School.

"I don't know," she said to Renee. "There seem to be a lot of extra steps in this Rounds process. The slow pace, filling out a formal Host Teacher Preparation Form with a colleague before each lesson, and the lengthy debrief meeting after the videoing—it all seems so cumbersome! And every group needs a facilitator with specific training, even if the teacher is a veteran with coaching experience. Our teachers are all very good—they don't need facilitators. I think the groups can run their own meetings."

Renee, who had been well taught at the summer workshop, understood that Rounds was no quick fix, and tried to push back against Claudia's concerns.

"Rounds takes time to implement," responded Renee. "And the facilitator is key to making the process productive in terms of improving student learning. It takes patience and persistence."

Claudia was not going to be persuaded. "Well, I think we can eliminate unnecessary steps and streamline the process. Then we can get up and running much more quickly and get faster results from the investment of time and energy. You can be the overall teacher leader/teacher facilitator and keep an eye on all the Rounds groups but not take full control. I want to create more leadership opportunities for teachers in the school. This is a good way to do it."

Renee was worried but knew she had no choice but to accept Claudia's decision. Rather than develop grade-level facilitators, Claudia assured her that the process would be more efficient if they "streamlined" it by starting out with a small group of grade-level representatives who would develop a "whole-school problem of practice."

Renee composed a detailed letter describing all the facets of the Rounds for Teachers process that she had learned during the summer, sent it to the entire faculty, and asked for volunteers to attend a planning meeting. She asked everyone, even those who wouldn't be attending the meeting, to develop some "wonderings" or ideas for the problem of practice prior to the meeting and to arrive ready to discuss their ideas.

In the meeting of the grade-level volunteers, each teacher shared his or her ideas for a problem of practice. Renee was surprised that many of the ideas the teachers had developed on their own were actually quite similar. Almost all the ideas proposed to the group dealt with writing skills or teacher scaffolding—or both.

After the teachers presented their ideas, Renee and Claudia helped narrow them down into one larger sentence, thinking out loud and asking the teachers for direction and feedback.

When the meeting was over, Renee and Claudia had two questions for the groups' problem of practice; both were instructional issues that transcended grade level and discipline: First, how are writing assignments (short assignments requiring a topic sentence, evidence, and explanations) presented, scaffolded, and executed in classes? And, second, how consistent are the written expectations and outcomes across the grade level?

Sylvia Robledo, the 3rd-grade teacher rep, left the meeting feeling energized. "The e-mail Renee sent us helped all of us think about our problems of practice, and the small group that Renee led gave us a good start on naming and getting started on solving the problem."

Choosing Lessons for the Rounds

With the goal of whole-school involvement, Renee and Claudia designed a Rounds format that would divide the entire faculty into four groups and provide multiple video clips for the first Faculty Rounds session. To make this happen, Renee videoed many lessons and highlighted potential clips for the Round.

Then Claudia and Renee selected four videos from different grade levels and took 10-minute clips from each of them. The clips highlighted the same issue but cut across different grade levels. The four teachers whose videos were chosen were pleased, and Claudia told them to bring samples of student work to the meeting.

Renee wondered who was really doing the work here. She was deciding on the clips, and the teachers were being told what student work to bring. She worried that this was getting more and more distant from the original intent of teacher leadership that had been so appealing to her in the summer workshop.

The Rounds Day

On the whole-school Rounds day, Claudia and Renee created four groups of teachers by mixing teachers from all grade levels. To each of the four groups, they distributed video-clip summaries they had developed and the copies of student work that corresponded with the clips. Renee led the meeting. She reviewed the Rounds process protocol, with its three-column chart, with the entire faculty, demonstrating how to look for teacher and student moves—and stating strongly that the teachers had to avoid making judgmental statements about the videos. Each of the four groups was voluntarily "facilitated" by one of the grade-level teachers who had attended the first meeting with Claudia and Renee, and one of the videoed teachers was present in each group.

After observing the videos and discussing what they had observed, the teachers quickly identified three major topics. First, how can we push students to explain evidence? Second, how can we reduce formulaic writing or rely on formulas in general? Third, regarding transfer of knowledge (across grade level or within the same subject), how can we teach students to activate prior knowledge within a content area so that written responses are more fully developed?

Next, the teachers brainstormed solutions to the problems, listed the ideas on chart paper, examined the solutions, and completed an "exit ticket" explaining strategies they would attempt in their classes to reach the solutions developed during the Round. Each group then reported out to the entire faculty and left the meeting with a set of potential solutions to the faculty's problems. The teachers were happy to have accomplished so much in just one meeting and were pleased with the commitments they had made.

Renee was complimented by almost all the teachers, who left the meeting energized. "That was the very best PD meeting I've ever attended," beamed 3rd-grade teacher Joan Stone. "I never realized that other people had the same problems that I had with writing instruction, and there they were, right on video—and we left the meeting with solutions! How often do we ever leave a meeting with a solution? And a teacher led it all. WOW."

"This is great," Yolanda said with a smile. "I feel so encouraged and excited. I feel in control. We'll make this happen."

But despite the energy of the teachers, Renee was troubled. "If we go so fast," she thought to herself, "will there be time for teachers to reflect on how these changes are going to affect their practice in connection to the instructional core?"

She understood that to change practice, the three parts of the instructional core needed to be changed. There had to be a change in the role of the student, in the content, and the teacher. Looking at the ideas listed on chart paper and listening to the exit cards, she noticed that all the changes were going to be things the *teacher* would do differently (e.g., "Tell kids to prove their evidence," "Teachers have to keep asking 'why?' until the student has come to conclusion/explanation,"

"Keep asking 'so what?' until . . ."). The only strategy that was child-centered was "Let kids struggle: Don't tell them how."

Second Semester

As the year raced along, teachers began to feel uncomfortable with their new PD, and Renee knew it as soon as she heard the first grumblings.

James Pak, one of the 5th-grade teachers, complained to Renee, "I've tried so many of our strategies, but I don't see the kids making progress."

Yolanda videoed herself and had other teachers at the 5th-grade level use the Rounds for Teachers protocol to comment on the video during a grade-level meeting, but she left the meeting dissatisfied. "Now what?" Yolanda asked herself. "I'm trying to implement the strategies, and I don't see any difference in the writing. And the rest of the team feels as stuck as I do."

"I really liked the Rounds meetings with the whole school, and I was struck how the problem of practice crossed grade levels," commented 4th-grade teacher Shanna Stigler, "but now that we're trying to implement the idea, it's much harder than we thought. How much better off are we now than we were before? Our meetings are descending into complaint sessions again. How can we use the protocols better? What's missing?"

What Happens Next?

As Renee looks back over the year, after hearing Yolanda's disappointment, she thinks back on her Rounds training and has a sense of why the teachers haven't bought into the process. Yes, the teams were managing on their own, the videos had demonstrated how the same problem of practice was prevalent across all grade levels, and the cross-grade emphasis with the particular problem had great potential—but they'd skipped important pieces of the process.

What could she do now? How should she present the truth to Claudia, and would Claudia listen?

CASE 3 GUIDE TO ANALYSIS

Key concept: Anxious to put responsibility for professional development into the hands of teachers by getting Rounds up and running quickly, an elementary school principal "streamlines" the process, with mixed results.

Step 1: Read the Case (10 minutes)

Distribute the teaching case and have the group read it through, underlining or highlighting pieces of information they think are significant to understanding the case.

Step 2: Establish the Facts of the Case (10 minutes)

As a whole group, make a list on chart paper of the significant "facts" of the teaching case. Include what you know about each team member. Try to withhold judgment, inferences, or evaluation, and come to agreement about what happened.

Step 3: Address the Issue of Principal Control and the Dilemma of the Quick Fix

Moving too quickly and skipping steps can cause problems. This is not an uncommon phenomenon in schools. Principals are under pressure to make changes that will help professional development work efficiently, produce visible improvements in teaching, and improve test scores, with all due speed. Schools maintain their old mantras: "We should be able to solve our problems efficiently." "There must be a shortcut!" "Change shouldn't take a long time."

Consider these questions:

1. Look over the case and underline places where the process was short-circuited. What were the consequences? What might Renee have done at those points?

2. When have you experienced a "speed-up" process in your school? What was the result?

3. How can teachers convince their bosses (principals, superintendents, and school boards) to adopt systems such as Rounds for Teachers that develop slowly and carefully but can make significant changes in curriculum and instruction that truly last?

PART III

Principals and Department Chairs

8

Role of the Principal

Understand What Rounds Requires

If you are a principal or head of school for whom building strong Rounds groups in your school is an attractive idea, or if you already have Rounds groups in your school and are looking for ways to help make them more effective, we welcome you to the club. Luckily, it is no longer very exclusive.

And now, a few words about the importance of good leadership:

A strong school leader models the change she or he asks of the faculty and staff. Modeling for faculty what Rounds asks of them is the single most important role a principal can play in the development of Rounds.

Rounds asks teachers to be ongoing learners. In turn, the principal must be a learner and be seen as a learner. Rounds asks teachers to make themselves vulnerable for the sake of improvement. So the principal must be willing to hear feedback. Rounds asks teachers to commit to change their work practice. The principal must make similar commitments.

Rounds asks teachers to provide one another with serious, nonjudgmental, evidence-based feedback. The principal needs to provide such feedback regularly for teachers, and make it clear that such feedback is not connected to any formal evaluation process.

Principals understand, in theory, the value of teachers working collaboratively with the goal of improved instruction. But hierarchical, top-down leadership from the principal isn't going to get the job done. If the model of distributed leadership isn't embraced by the principal, then the goal of building strong, effective Rounds groups (which are, in effect, teacher teams) will remain an unfulfilled dream.

The following tasks, for example, are critical practical components of support over which the principal can exert leadership in concert with the administrative team and teachers:

- Finding the right talent to start and maintain Rounds, particularly the initial group of facilitators and faculty
- Carving out time from the schedule for teachers to do the work and making that time sacred, letting nothing "bump" it for the teachers involved—*which means synchronizing planning periods with Rounds meeting times*
- Spending personal time leading the program strategically and symbolically, perhaps by covering classes for teachers in Rounds
- Providing needed financial support for stipends or consultants, if needed
- Being ready and available to intervene personally to solve problems when the inevitable problems arise

Assess Teacher Talent

Again, it cannot be said too often that the principal needs to find opportunities to engage teachers and teacher leaders in the process of building strong Rounds groups. Creating a preliminary Rounds committee, for example, staffed with volunteers who express an interest in getting Rounds groups off the ground might be a good place to start.

Who can serve as Rounds group facilitators? Look for the teachers who

- are respected by other faculty,
- have skills in observing teaching,
- have the temperament suited for a facilitator (good listening skills, good social cognition, not overbearing, good collaborator, not afraid to push people gently), and

- understand that teacher leadership as exerted through Rounds facilitation is a delicate cultural process of balancing authority and collegiality.

In the interactions between the principal and the Rounds group, the facilitator is at the center of the action . . . and it's in the principal's best interest to make sure that it remains so. The skilled facilitator is the glue between the principal and the Rounds group (see Figure 8.1).

Choose the Best Candidates

Who will be best at participating in Teacher Rounds as it starts?

- Teachers who are willing to participate in Rounds—and desire to improve teaching practice
- Teachers who are not on any improvement plan (i.e., those who are secure in their jobs)
- Teachers whose participation will reinforce the credibility of the Rounds process for administrators and other teachers

Lay the Cultural Groundwork

- School leaders (principal, assistant principal, deans, department chairs) should regularly observe and give teachers explicit feedback that is focused on teacher growth. Make it clear that this feedback is unconnected to evaluation.
- Spend time talking to small groups of teachers about plans for Rounds, collect their concerns, and then address these as the plans for Rounds to continue to develop.

Figure 8.1 Principal–Facilitator–Rounds Group Relationship

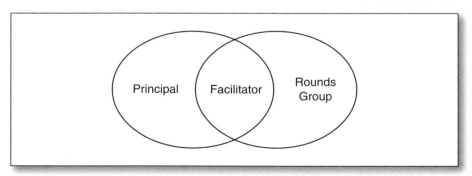

Build on Firm Ground With Good Resources

Getting a school ready for Rounds involves two core tasks: finding the right people to construct the program by identifying the teacher leadership skills already present in the school and preparing firm ground for Rounds to rest on by building a sense of trust around host teacher observations. Each of these involves a commitment of time on the part of school leaders to observe classes, give feedback, and have conversations with teachers about the role of observation for growth.

The more that school leaders demonstrate a commitment to teacher growth that is unconnected to evaluation, the more naturally Rounds will fit into the school culture. Identifying the teachers with the skills, beliefs, and dispositions for participating or facilitating Rounds allows schools to leverage the talent already present to get Rounds off to a successful start. Over time, Rounds will build more and more teacher capacity for its expansion.

Provide Ongoing Support

Build into the plans time for reflection and mutual support among those planning, running, and facilitating Rounds. This might include an outside coach/consultant with experience in running a successful Rounds program.

Although it is a challenge to find the time, some principals create and support facilitator study groups where facilitators have the opportunity to learn from each other.

Video: A Principal Comments on the Value of Teacher Rounds

 V8.1 A Principal Committed to Teacher Growth (2 mins.)

In this video, a K–8 elementary school principal, who has been invited to sit in on a Rounds group, demonstrates her commitment to teacher growth and risk taking.

9

Rounds for Department Chairs

Improving High School Teacher Development and Supervision

Department Chairs Step Up

A department chair is someone who has administrative responsibilities for an academic discipline. The chair may oversee curriculum development for the department and, frequently, may also have evaluative responsibilities for the teachers in his or her department. It is generally assumed that most department chairs are also teachers who have their own classes, but it is rare to find a department chair in the role of "teacher developer."

A teacher developer is anyone tasked with helping teachers improve their teaching practice. That is most often the role of a mentor, a Rounds facilitator, a peer coach, or an administrator, such as a dean of faculty or an assistant principal.

Our belief is that department chairs ought to be charged with the responsibility of being teacher developers, and in that role they need to be actively engaged in the improvement of their own practice to acquire the skills and knowledge to be able to do that effectively.

No professional is exempt from the ongoing process of continuing improvement of professional practice—not doctors or lawyers or teachers or, as we have proposed, principals and heads of schools. Department chairs—you're next.

Department Chair Rounds flows from the belief that department chairs are uniquely situated to be effective teacher developers and should see being a teacher developer as a critical part, perhaps even the main part, of their work as department chairs.

Pull the Lever

Quality of teaching is the single most powerful lever for improving student learning. In high schools, that lever rests in the hands of department chairs, and Department Chair Rounds can be an effective fulcrum for using that lever.

Department chairs typically have

- administrative skills,
- mastery of content area, and
- excellent teaching skills in the classroom.

Department chairs typically lack

- experience or skill in observing others teach,
- skill in giving useful and appropriate feedback, and
- skill in helping teachers form long-term goals for pedagogy.

Department Chair Rounds (DCR) is designed to develop these critical skills.

DCR rests on these core assumptions:

1. The primary job of a department chair should be teacher development.

2. Department chairs are in the best position to improve teaching throughout a high school.

3. Department chairs can significantly improve their skills in developing their teachers *only* **by observing and analyzing each other** working with teachers on teaching.

Both observing a class and debriefing an observation of a teacher can be fast-paced, fraught with problems, and require quick decisions in the moment. Department Chair Rounds allows chairs the chance to analyze that complicated work, to slow things down, to see their work with teachers "from the outside"—all of which will make the process easier the next time.

The Difference Between Faculty Rounds and Department Chair Rounds

Faculty Rounds is a peer-facilitated process of observation and analysis of teaching practice, focused on a single area of teaching practice for a year. A "host teacher" each month describes his or her specific problem of practice, invites the Rounds group to a particular class, and details what the other teachers in the Rounds group should observe. The group members then meet to share data from the observation, consider things they wonder about that were stimulated by the observation, and then make commitments to small changes in their own teaching before the next Rounds meeting. The protocols rule out problem solving and advice; the purpose is to stimulate *critical analysis* about teaching. By coming to their own conclusions and committing to small, manageable changes in teaching practice, teachers can see long-term improvements.

Department Chair Rounds differs from Faculty Rounds in its focus on the specific skills of *developing teachers in their departments*—observing, giving feedback, conducting an effective conference, and forming a plan for the development of a teacher. The primary observation is not in a classroom but, rather, of the video of a department chair's post-observation conference with the teacher. The "host department chair" describes a specific problem of practice he or she has in helping teachers improve and indicates what the other chairs should look for in the video of the post-observation conference. As in Faculty Rounds, the group then meets to share data and "wonderings," without offering advice or trying to solve one another's problems. The goal is for the department chairs to come to their own understanding of how to improve the development of teachers.

DCR is not focused on the chairs' own teaching practice. Instead, it focuses on building the department chairs' capacity to improve the practice of the *teachers* in their departments.

Most department chairs teach and also want to continue to improve their own teaching practice in their classes. But DCR is not for that purpose.

DCR aims at improving department chairs' skills in their capacity as teacher developers: observing teachers, giving useful feedback, and helping teachers form teaching goals.

In practical terms, the biggest difference is this: The heart of DCR is a video recording of the department chair's post-observation conference with the teacher who was observed. To prepare for the Round, the host department chair videos the teacher's class and his or her own debrief with that teacher. The two videos are put on the department chair conference site. Prior to meeting, the Rounds group of department chairs observes those videos as homework and then meets to analyze and reflect on how the host department chair handled the post-observation conference.

How to Implement Department Chair Rounds

Figure 9.1 Department Chair Rounds Cycle

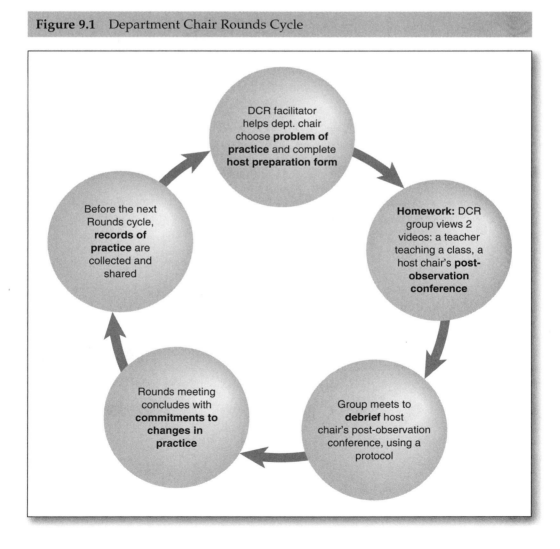

1. Prepare the host.

   The DCR group facilitator works with the host department chair on defining a problem of practice that is observable, actionable, and significant. The Department Chair Rounds Host Preparation Form (Figure 9.2) sent to the other chairs ahead of the observation should specify what to look for in the post-observation conference and what data to collect.

2. Homework: In preparation for the Round, DCR group participants view two videos.

   a. The teacher teaching the class

   b. The host department chair conducting a post-observation conference

3. Debrief the post-observation conference.

   The DCR group members meet to analyze their observations according to the protocol (Figure 9.4).

4. Commit to a change of practice.

   Based on what has been learned from the observation, each department chair commits to a small, doable change in his or her work with teachers.

5. Share records of practice.

   The next Rounds meeting begins by sharing records of practice that show the changes department chairs attempted to implement with their faculty as a result of Rounds.

Build a Culture of Trust

Department Chair Rounds must be built on a solid foundation of trust. Teachers need to feel comfortable being observed and recorded. Department chairs need to feel comfortable being seen on video by other chairs as they work with a teacher. DCR creates trust as chairs signal to their teachers that they are learners, too, that they are willing to expose their own practice, and that they take these risks to better support their teachers.

Key elements to developing and improving a culture of trust through DCR include the following:

- The Rounds work is supported and rewarded by the principal.
- Adherence to protocols makes DCR safe for chairs and teachers—no chair should talk outside the Rounds group about anything he or she saw of the teacher's work.
- The chairs begin work with the most confident, well-respected teachers, demonstrating that the program isn't seeking out problem teachers.
- Teachers are allowed to opt out if they don't feel comfortable having their post-observation conferences videoed.

Select Your DCR Facilitator

Each DCR group needs a facilitator—an experienced department chair or other teacher developer (such as an assistant principal)—to frame the whole process for the group, to facilitate the Rounds meetings to make sure the protocols are followed, and to help the host chairs each month prepare their Department Chair Rounds Host Preparation Form.

Facilitator Frames Rounds

To focus on building the department chairs' capacity to improve the practice of the *teachers* in their departments, DCR has two overall aims: to improve department chairs' skills in

1. observing teachers and

2. giving effective feedback.

Achieving these aims rests on some fundamental understandings:

- Rounds is not a place to talk about teachers, only about the department chairs' practice as teacher developers.
- Rounds must adapt to the needs of all the department chairs.
- Each DCR participant is a learner with different strengths and weaknesses.
- This is a slow process of small improvements; department chairs must be patient with one another.

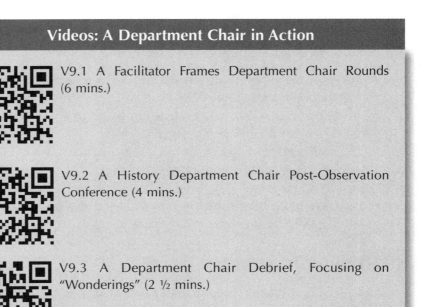

Videos: A Department Chair in Action

V9.1 A Facilitator Frames Department Chair Rounds (6 mins.)

V9.2 A History Department Chair Post-Observation Conference (4 mins.)

V9.3 A Department Chair Debrief, Focusing on "Wonderings" (2 ½ mins.)

You can see how the facilitator of one DCR group frames Rounds in Video V9.1, a post-observation conference in Video V9.2, and a department chair debrief in Video V9.3.

Prepare the Department Chair Host

Part of the role of facilitator is to help prepare the host department chair. Each month in Department Chair Rounds, one member of the group, on a rotating basis, will be the host chair. This allows every member of the group to benefit from observation and feedback about his or her practice. The host chair defines a problem of practice in his or her work developing teachers and tells the group what to look for in the Department Chair Rounds Host Preparation Form (Figure 9.2). The host chair videos the class of a teacher with whom he or she is working and then videos the post-observation conference with that teacher, making both videos available to the entire DCR group before the monthly meeting. Defining the problem of practice, and then basing the Rounds discussion on a real observation, grounds the discussion in the actual practice of trying to develop teachers.

It is important to keep in mind that the focus of Department Chair Rounds isn't the teacher's class; it is *the chair's conference with the teacher.* Thus, the Department Chair Rounds Host Preparation Form must highlight a specific **problem of practice** that the **host chair** is working on: for example, skills of observation, skills in giving good feedback, or skills in developing a plan of growth for a teacher. The Department Chair Rounds Host Preparation Form must specify what to look for in the post-observation conference. It also must let the group know what the chair is observing in the teacher's class so that when the other department chairs observe the teacher, they look for the same thing.

Choose a Compelling Problem of Practice

With help from the facilitator, host chairs must determine something they have found challenging about trying to help a given teacher improve. The area of challenge should be something that is

Figure 9.2   Department Chair Rounds Host Preparation Form

| [Name] | [Date, Time, Location of class to be observed] |
| | [Date video of debriefing with teacher will be available] |

Challenge of Practice

What is it about observing my teachers or giving them useful feedback that I find a compelling, unresolved question? This isn't about structural impediments (e.g., teaching the same blocks as another teacher, making it hard to get into her class), and it isn't about the teacher (e.g., this teacher is resistant to feedback). Rather, this about something you have still not worked out about how to observe or give feedback.

Context for the Observation

Background on the class, the material to be covered in that lesson, **the relevant teaching goals you are using to work with that teacher, your plan for your own observation of the class**. In addition, you will be conducting a post-observation conference with the teacher that you will video, so you need to tell us something about your **goals for that debriefing and your plan for how to achieve those goals**.

Focus and Method of Observation for Other Department Chairs

Focus of Observation	*Method of Observation*
What we should look for in the teacher's class and in your debrief with the teacher. When it comes to the debrief, the focus needs to be about what YOU are doing, the moves you are making to help the teacher.	• Be specific about what you would like us to observe—for example, are my questions open or leading? Am I prompting the teacher to think things through for him-or herself or giving advice? • If you have a second suggested method of observation or data collection, list it, but two seems about as many as people can handle.
You might have a second or a secondary focus for the group.	• Again, list HOW we are to observe for this focus.

within the chair's control, that the chair could act on, that is observable when the chair meets with the teacher, and that is strongly connected to teacher learning.

Examples of Poorly Formulated Problems of Practice

- I worry the teacher acts differently when I observe and isn't as effective when I'm not there.
- It is hard to find time to observe enough classes of a teacher I am worried about; I can't give her consistent help.
- How do I know if what I am looking for is the right thing?
- I worry about how teachers will feel being observed; that hasn't happened in my department.

In each of these cases, the chair is naming a real concern. Yet none of these is a well-formulated problem of practice for a department chair in the role of teacher developer to work on. Nothing can be done about the effects of observing or the lack of time. Not knowing what to look for isn't a problem of practice yet—but it could be turned into a problem about the skill of diagnosing that changes in a teacher's practice could yield the biggest jump in student learning. Likewise, the last observation could be restated in terms of what the *chair* can do—namely, how to deliver feedback in such a way that teachers are not defensive; that is a skill worth developing, and it is critical for chairs to be able to develop their teachers.

Examples of Well-Formulated Problems of Practice

- How do I determine whether to take a more directive or more collaborative stance with a teacher?
- How do I conduct a more directive conference with a teacher, particularly where the teacher doesn't understand the issue in his or her teaching?
- What approaches can I use to help a teacher who seems to understand what he or she needs to work on, can make successful experiments with new techniques, but doesn't seem able to make the improvements a habitual part of his or her teaching practice?
- How can I help a teacher who is talented in a narrow range of teaching modalities realize the value of expanding his or her repertoire when the new modalities never seem to work as well as the old, comfortable ones?
- How do I make sure there is a clear plan moving forward after each debriefing, and that the teacher understands that plan?

Each of these is a substantial problem of practice for the chair and focuses on what is within the chair's capacity to control (notice that the word "I" appears in each).

Prepare for the Round

There is no substitute for preparation. It is a well-worn cliché that preparation is 50% of the work, but it is well-worn for a good reason. No enterprise can be fully successful without it. To use the limited time available for department meetings as productively as possible, department chairs must first watch the video of a teacher teaching a class and then a video of the host chair conducting the post-conference observation with the teacher.

To see a typical example of how this is done, watch the video of a history department chair's post-observation conference with the 10th-grade history teacher (Video V9.2). Prior to watching the video, look at the completed example of the Department Chair Rounds Host Preparation Form (Figure 9.3).

Figure 9.3   Example Department Chair Rounds Host Preparation Form

Yoni _____ History Chair	Tues. Nov. 13, C Block, 9th-grade Western Civ. (videoed) Class video will be available by Wed. Nov. 14 in the PM Debrief video will be available Thurs. Nov. 15

Challenge of Practice

How do Joanna and I work toward her goal of creating more open spaces in her classroom for the kids to do the intellectual heavy lifting on a more organic "on-the-spot" basis (as opposed to designed seminars and the like)? My challenge in helping Joanna has two key components:

1. How do I use my observations of Joanna to diagnose the stumbling blocks for/with her in making substantive changes in this area?
2. How do I devise a "curriculum" for my work with Joanna (i.e., what are the steps in my work with Joanna) to get her to the goal I have in my supervision of her?

Context for the Observation

Classroom:

Joanna's goal for this class is to help the students review the skill of creating a strong historical claim. The steps include creating a working claim; finding

(Continued)

Figure 9.3   (Continued)

evidence for that claim from a primary source; analyzing the evidence; finding a common idea from evidence; and then refining working claim.

For homework (due for this class) Joanna gave the students a scaffolded worksheet that posed an overarching historical question and then asked the students to create a historical claim using the steps enumerated above. In this class Joanna planned on having the students review these various skills.

Joanna's plan to achieve this goal was to have the students practice using these skills (during the class). Students would share a piece of evidence they found for homework (preferably one not discovered by many of the other students) and then use that evidence to practice each of the skills. Students should be at the fore of explaining how to apply each of the skills.

In my observation, I will be looking for the occasions in which Joanna opens space (or missed chances to open space) in her classroom for the kids to do the intellectual heavy lifting. What questions or tasks does Joanna pose that open opportunities for explorations by the students? Does Joanna allow time for students to pursue those explorations? Does she allow many students to explore a given line of inquiry before ending it or intervening with her own take on the issue? Does Joanna help create habits of independent thinking by, for example, asking other students to respond to one another, or letting students determine the direction of the conversation, or encouraging students to analyze one another's views?

Debrief:

The meeting will begin by my asking Joanna to explore some of the opportunities she leveraged in opening analytical conversation carried by the students. We will next observe a video clip or two from the class (selected by me) and unpack the choices Joanna made in those moments. Finally, we will together devise and agree upon Joanna's next step (something she will try in an upcoming class).

Focus and Method of Observation for Other Department Chairs

Focus of Observation	*Method of Observation*
Classroom Observation: Look for examples of ways that Joanna provides space for the students to explore generative questions (or does not) and ways in which Joanna empowers the students to be the intellectual "heavy lifters" of the class learning. 1. **Asking and opening:** Does Joanna pose open and generative questions for the students and then allow them the time to answer them without her comments or interventions?	In each of these cases, please use **scripting** of the class— write down what Joanna or students say or questions that are asked that seem relevant to these three areas. Please keep your notes to what is actually observed, not judgments or inferences about what you are seeing.

Focus of Observation	Method of Observation
2. **Recognizing and availing:** Where may there be opportunities to open the floor to intellectual heavy lifting by the kids? Does Joanna open the floor to those questions—that is, does she encourage the class to follow lines of inquiry suggested by students? 3. **Where is the focus?** Who is the focal point of the learning? To whom do the students speak, and to whom do they respond?	
Teacher Debrief Observation: In what ways do I use evidence from the class observation or from what Joanna says in the debrief to diagnose any stumbling blocks for Joanna? How explicit and clear am I with Joanna about that diagnosis? In what ways do I work with Joanna to frame the next step in her work on the basis of that diagnosis? Am I clear about the next step—what we are working on, what is expected of Joanna, what we will be looking for in a future observation?	**Using Scripting:** 1. What evidence do you see that I am helping Joanna diagnose stumbling blocks to progress? 2. In what ways do I use evidence from the class observation to reach an understanding with Joanna about what we need to work on next (i.e., the diagnosis of a stumbling block). 3. What do you see that suggests clarity or lack of clarity on my part about the next step? In what ways have I checked that Joanna understands the next step?

As you watch the video (V9.2), pay particular attention to

- the department chair's effort to focus the teacher on the goal of having students do more of the intellectual work and
- the department chair's attempt to help the teacher visualize what active engagement by the students would look like to help move the teacher from a teacher-centered class to a more student-centered class.

Follow the Protocol for Debriefing

It is critical that the DCR meeting stay focused on *the chair's work* as a teacher developer and not shift back to the teacher. The purpose of the debriefing protocol (Figure 9.4) is to provide a sense of *safety* for the host, push members to *analyze* instead of offering advice, and keep the *focus* of the discussion where it should be—on the host chair's problem of practice.

Figure 9.4 Department Chair Rounds Debriefing Protocol

1. Honoring Commitments

Review briefly what you have done since the meeting the previous month, and share records of practice showing evidence of that commitment.

2. Sharing Observations

Host chair shares reflections on the teacher observation and debriefing: Review the goals for the teacher and to what extent those seem met, where there were difficulties in meeting those goals.

Observations from the rest of the group: Descriptions of what we observed about the host chair's problem of practice (remember, it is about the chair's work, not the teacher). The most important aspect of this is that it needs to be descriptive, not evaluative.

3. Wonderings/Open, Honest Questions

What do you genuinely wonder about in what you saw in the host chair's work? These are questions about the chair, not the teacher or students, and like open, honest questions, they should not have preambles, they should not be disguised advice, and you should not have a particular answer in mind. The point is not to offer solutions but to stimulate thinking.

4. Selective Response by Host Chair

Respond to what seems most relevant to the problem of practice, extend a wondering, and so on.

5. Learning

Each person will describe something he or she has learned from the observation and debrief.

6. Commitments

Each session, on the basis of the observation and learnings, department chairs commit to one small change in their practice with observing/giving feedback to teachers.

Watch the Video

Video V9.3 shows an example of "wonderings" during a Round to keep the focus on analysis and reflection rather than advice. Note that the host chair records the wonderings rather than responding.

Practice Your Post-Observation Conference End Game

Experience suggests that department chairs should formulate one or two commitments for the entire year, rather than change their commitments every month. The end game is one such core skill that can serve as a year-long commitment. By "end game" we mean finishing a post-observation conference so as to properly set up the ongoing work with a teacher. Does the teacher leave the post-observation conference with an understanding of what aspects of his or her teaching practice to work on and how that work is to proceed? Too often, department chairs and teachers leave the post-observation conference with very different understandings of what just took place and what should happen next. Having a strong end game ensures that this does not happen.

Make an End-Game Checklist

At the end of the post-observation conference, the chair commits to making sure there is a clear, mutual understanding between the chair and the teacher about

> ✓ the problem of teaching practice the chair wants the teacher to work on,
> ✓ what the next action items are for the teacher,
> ✓ when those next steps need to be done,
> ✓ what records of practice need to be kept,
> ✓ when the next observation will take place, and
> ✓ when the next post-observation conference will take place.

It can be helpful to reserve time during a Rounds meeting to role-play the end game. Have participants break into pairs, with one chair playing the role of a specific teacher with whom the other chair plans to meet. Practice going through the checklist with a "teacher" who doesn't quite understand what is expected. Then switch roles. Role playing can be used several times a year to practice core skills that many in the group seem to need.

PART IV

Appendices

Appendix A

CCSS Speaking and Listening Standards 6–12

Initiate and participate effectively in a range of collaborative discussions (one-on-one, in groups, and teacher-led) with diverse partners, building on others' ideas and expressing their own clearly and persuasively.

   a. Come to discussions prepared, having read and researched material under study; explicitly draw on that preparation by referring to evidence from texts and other research on the topic or issue to stimulate a thoughtful, well-reasoned exchange of ideas.

   b. Work with peers to promote civil, democratic discussions and decision making; set clear goals and deadlines; and establish individual roles as needed.

   c. Propel conversations by posing and responding to questions that probe reasoning and evidence; ensure a hearing for a full range of positions on a topic or issue; clarify, verify, or challenge ideas and conclusions; and promote divergent and creative perspectives.

   d. Respond thoughtfully to diverse perspectives; synthesize comments, claims, and evidence made on all sides of an issue; resolve contradictions when possible; and determine what additional information or research is required to deepen the investigation or complete the task.

Appendix B

Glenda's Host Teacher Preparation Form

Name: Glenda Solas   **Date of Round:** Monday, September 30, 2013 (1:40–2:35)

1. Review/explain problem of practice

How can teachers keep students engaged and facilitate critical thinking among and between students to make the subject matter meaningful?

I worry that my students do not grapple in any meaningful way with the issues presented in this lesson, and I wonder how to obtain greater student ownership of the material so that their own critical engagement will enhance their learning.

I am interested in assessing how engaged the students are with the material, and how long they are able to keep their focus as we move through the material and from one activity to another. This is also a class where it is difficult for me to interpret their demeanor—they can often look bored and disconnected and then suddenly become a part of the conversation. The question for me is, when they appear less engaged—are they really disconnected, or simply trying to understand the material we are discussing? These are some of my measures for student engagement: raising their hands, eye contact, note-taking, nodding, asking questions of their classmates, challenging opinions of others, and following along with the material. I would like to know how I can increase sustained engagement of all the students in the class, especially when they work with one another.

I am wondering whether the quieter students are feeling intimidated to speak up or are simply unsure of the material. Is this a class in which they feel comfortable taking chances? (This is not a data-driven question—just a wondering about the reasons behind lack of engagement.)

2. Provide context for the lesson

This class is the heart of the case study that we have been leading up to this year. We will be discussing the political dominance of Caesar Augustus. The kids will come in with background on not just the period but also Augustus himself.

The skills focus of this lesson is application of evidence/claim and analysis. The students have been working on both the identification and the production of "good" pieces of evidence and claims since September. This is the first time I will be adding in the idea of analysis.

First, I will review the content—so we all are working from the same background. We are discussing their homework, which was to read primary source material. To some extent, the amount of time we will have to get into the actual skill activity will depend on how comfortable the students feel with this primary source. The review of this will be in recitation style. I will leave open a period of time for them to ask for specific help on the homework. I will also ask one or two specific questions to ensure that they have the basic idea with which to move forward in the lesson.

Second, they will break up into pairs and we will go through first a reading and summarization activity and then an evidence/claim skill activity. Directions for both activities will be projected on the Smart Board. They will proceed to read and summarize more of the primary source material together. They will be using a specific method for doing the summarization that carries over from their homework. They will already have this on a worksheet in their homework packet.

Having completed the worksheet, they will move onto the claim/evidence activity, which will focus on their ability both to find evidence to support a claim and to refine a working claim.

Third, after about 15 minutes, I will introduce this new idea of analysis into the creation of the evidence/claim skill. This will move the students back from pair work to frontal teaching. I will review what analysis means and how it fits into claim and evidence. As a class, we will complete one example together before they add this new component into the content of their pair work.

For all parts of this lesson, I will have two ways of assessing their understanding: through discussion/questions and through the written material they will hand in.

3. On what should the observers focus their attention?

I would like observers to focus on student engagement through students' questions, comments, and demeanor (raising their hands, eye contact, note-taking, nodding, asking questions of their class-mates, and following along with the material) during the time I am in front of the classroom, as well as their conversation with one another when they are in pairs. How do they respond to my different moves (wait time, cold calling, verbal reminders to participate)? Are they less likely to become engaged unless I call on them?

I am having students work with partners whom they have worked with recently, as I believe these pairs work well together. Are they focused? Are they learning and helping each other? Are they pushing each other? I'd appreciate if you could divide up and take notes on what students are saying in their pairs. Then we could analyze whether it constitutes "critical thinking."

4. To what extent should/would you like observers to interact with students?

Feel free to interact with students during partner time. In general, process questions are encouraged, but I'd avoid questions specific to content, especially any with pedagogical intent.

Determine what additional information or research is required to deepen the investigation or complete the task.

Appendix C

Glenda's Record of Practice

Objective: I used a summarizer to check for understanding of both:
  1. Skills:
      a. Note-taking
          i. Are they taking the kinds of notes that will actually enable them to gain an understanding of the larger picture?
      b. What constitutes evidence
          i. Are they able to identify clear pieces of good evidence?
          ii. Does their evidence actually support a claim?
      c. Analyzing evidence
          i. Do they really understand the evidence?
          ii. Can they provide both explanation and connection for the evidence?

*** The skill of analyzing evidence has proved to be a very difficult one to teach. Some kids just get it intuitively, but most do not. The idea behind this was to break down this process for them.

  2. Content:
      a. Understanding how the problems, both internal and external problems, actually hurt the Roman Empire.
      b. Understanding how the problems collectively could destroy the empire.

- The Students came into class with reading and notes from 2 nights of hw.
- The students were familiar with all of the skills that I was checking.
- They were most familiar with the ideas of evidence.
- The note-taking was assigned to be completed by using the method of claim/evidence. It was a new method for me to try as well.
- As a class we had gone over the idea of evidence analyzing but this was the first in-class assignment asking them to do this.

Directions: Using the evidence from your notes prove or disprove one of the following claims:

During the 3rd century the internal problems of the Western Roman Empire allowed for various barbarians tribes to invade and ultimately dominate Europe.

OR

Despite the fact that the Germanic tribes sought Rome's protection, they ultimately caused additional destruction to the weakened empire.

1.   Choose at least 2 specific pieces of evidence.

2.   Explain each piece of evidence
     Include why each piece of evidence proves or disproves the claim.

Findings:

Out of 10 - only 1 used the second claim.
     The first claim related to a reading that had much more evidence. Also, the evidence was more familiar to them and seemed more straightforward. (Which is why out of the all the evidence to choose from, they all, individually chose the same ones).

**They all understood (on some level) what I was asking them to do.

(A)   Applying the content, no matter how straightforward, to more ambitious skills really brought out how confused and jumbled some ideas were in their heads.

(B)   Have a somewhat superficial understanding of the ideas – which makes it very difficult to provide coherent analysis

(C)   Do not have a complete understanding of the argument/counterargument (i.e., does mercenary necessarily mean disloyal?)

(D)   Making huge leaps between the facts (evidence) and the claim. Cannot connect the dots.

(E)   Lack of understanding of how to create an argument out of facts

During the 3rd century, the internal problems of the Western Roman Empire allowed for various barbarians tribes to invade and ultimately dominate Europe.

A.

Evidence:

- In the 3rd century, there was a lack of loyalty in the military; soldiers were loyal to their individual commanders rather than Rome, and the roman government also hired foreign mercenaries.
    - This proves the claim because it shows that Rome was weakened and vulnerable. If the military wasn't as loyal to Rome, they wouldn't try so hard to protect the empire. Also, because of the weakness in the military, border patrol wasn't as strong which made it easier for invading tribes to enter.
- Rome experienced agriculture problems; soil was overworked (meaning it produced less food), war destroyed land, and the raise in taxes caused many farmers to leave their land.
    - When the Visigoths put Rome under siege, they cut off Rome's eternal food supply. Rome couldn't support itself under siege because off all the abandoned farms and the lack of food grown from overworked soil. They were starving to death, and they were forced to open the gate to the invaders.

B.

Evidence

In the milatery, Soldies lost tehir loyalty to Rome, and were only loyal to their Commamders

Rome became less united, when invaders attacked. Roman Soldier Cared more about thembselves and less about the City.

Because of the drop in Population in Rome, their werent enough Soldiers in the army.

Because the army was foreigners they Wouldn't Protect Rome.

C.

1. Rome began hiring foreign merceneries to fight in their army in the 3rd century C.E.

a. This proves the claim since the mercenaries had no loyalty to Rome and so had less of a drive to ~~defend~~ Rome, and many of them were Germanic This allowed Germanic barbarians to defeat the mercenaries in battle and invade Rome

2. From 235-284 CE, ~~because Romans were uninterested in politics,~~ Roman armies declared 50 generals to be emporers. 26 were approved by the Senate, but 25 were brutally murdered.

a. With no stable emporer the Roman government and army were in disorder since they had no commander-in-cheif to control the armies and defend Rome successfully.

1) By the 200s local officials usually lost Money because they were forced to pay for the costly public circuses and baths with their own Money, which made the officers job less desireable

They did not have a govelnment due to this, Which Means that they were un organized. They are not a functional City withought a govelnment, so Other countries would want to attack them.

E

Evidence:
1. lack of loyalty in military:
   - many mercenaries - weren't loyal to Rome (big % of army)
   - soldiers weren't fighting for Rome
2. vulnerable military
   - ~~Bosta~~ ~~threatened Roman too bay~~ foriegners over Roman teratton
   - ~~sieged~~
   - haven't been attacked by foriegners in 600 years

because there was lack of loyalty in the military this enabled invasion because mercenaries, a big percentage of the military, were not fighting for Rome and the soldiers were no longer fighting for Rome, but there for generatin Roman

Barbarians were able to invade because Rome was being threatened by foriegners and Rome had not been attacked in 600 years

Appendix D

Observation Workshop

Learning to See, Unlearning to Judge[1]

Content: Teaching the difference between description and interpretation

Essential question: How do we observe practice to improve learning and teaching?

Materials
• Rounds Observation Worksheet (Figure D.1) • A 10-minute video clip of a classroom observation (See Video VD.1 for a sample that you might want to use for this workshop.) • Chart paper and markers

Video: Observing a Classroom

 VD.1 Classroom Observation—Grade 3

Use this video with your group to practice observation skills, or you can use any other teaching video you prefer. The purpose of viewing the video is to learn how to observe teaching practice in a nonjudgmental way—a prerequisite for doing Rounds.

Step 1: Workshop Introduction

Facilitator's preparation: Generate your own answers to questions below.

Explain that one of the fundamental skills needed for productive classroom observation, a core skill of a successful Round, is the ability to differentiate between *description* and *interpretation*. Point out that observing practice doesn't happen in a vacuum and is not the end goal; we are learning *how to observe in the service of improving teaching and learning*.

Facilitate a conversation that includes the following:

- What is the difference between description and interpretation?
- What might be included in description?
- What might be included in interpretation?

Step 2: View the Video

Facilitator's preparation: View the video and complete the Rounds Observation Worksheet prior to the workshop

Distribute the Rounds Observation Worksheet (Figure D.1). Point out that there are three columns. Ask teachers to record as much as they can of what they *observe*. Caution participants that they are likely to watch the teacher more than the students, and encourage them to look instead for data about the students and the content being taught.

Emphasize that it is important that the data are not prematurely interpreted. Explain that this is a difficult skill to develop but extremely worthwhile if we understand that this kind of data-driven feedback can improve teaching and learning.

Figure D.1   Rounds Observation Worksheet

Teacher _____   .   Date _____

Problem of Practice _____

Teacher actions, quotes	Student names, actions, quotes	Questions/analyses

Reviewing the Rounds Observation Worksheet, highlight the following points:

1. There are three columns to ensure that you keep interpretations separate from descriptions.

2. Take as many literal notes as you can. Focus on factual observations.

3. Observational data should be specific, not general—objective, not interpretive.

4. Capture as many quotes as possible.

    a. In the left-hand column, record what the teacher is doing/saying.

    b. In the middle column, record what the students are doing/saying.

    c. In the right-hand column, write questions, analyses, or inferences separately.

Depending on the clip you choose, a possible focus for this observation could be as follows:

- What, if anything, is the teacher doing to create and maintain an effective environment for student learning?
- What, if anything, does he or she do to establish and reinforce expectations?

View the video (and include a short description of what is on the video).

Step 3: Debrief the Video

Facilitator's preparation: Read the
following and put in your own words

Introduce the idea that during group discussions you'll talk about the teacher as if she or he were in the room. Suggest that participants consider the teacher whose work is being examined to be a silent member of the group. If a teacher makes a negative remark about the teacher on the video, remind the group about the importance of treating the absent teacher with respect (again, as if he or she were "in the room") and help reframe the remark as a question. This will help build trust within your group when teachers are ready to share their own practice with the group.

After viewing the video, ask participants what they noticed about the lesson (referring to their worksheets). Reinforce the idea that the focus today is on *descriptive* comments as opposed to *interpretive* ones. All comments must be supported by evidence. There will be opportunities at a later time to make inferences or interpretations (an assumption supported by evidence).

If evaluative or interpretive statements are made, be sure to ask what data support that interpretation and encourage participants to rephrase an opinion as an objective statement. Explain that you are not suggesting that we never give opinions, but it is essential to always begin with the data. Record observations on chart paper.

Try to record data about the teacher, students, and task.

1. What did you notice about the teacher?

2. What did you notice about the students?

3. What did you notice about the task?

VERY IMPORTANT: Participants must stick to the facts *only*. There is a huge temptation, when analyzing classroom practice, for teachers to voice *opinions,* such as, "She talks too much during the class" or "The kids are not engaged." These are not *facts* but subjective *opinions,* and negative comments such as these are counterproductive. If teachers feel they will be attacked for opening up their practice for other teachers to view, they simply will not do it. Making practice public is a risky proposition, and part of your challenge as a facilitator is to ensure that teachers are able to trust that their practice will be viewed objectively and constructively.[2]

Step 4: Wrap-Up

Facilitator's preparation: Prepare answers to the following

1. Why is a focus on description so important as an observation skill?

2. What are some disadvantages of beginning with interpretation or judgment?

Facilitator: Before you convene the first Round, familiarize yourself with the next section about choosing a compelling problem of practice. That will be an important activity during your first round.

Appendix E

Example of a Problem of Practice Aligned to the Common Core State Standards

Let's take a look at teachers in a Grades 3–5 Teacher Rounds group in an urban school. They have identified a problem of practice, which they arrived at after agreeing that their math students "lack persistence and perseverance in using mathematical discourse." After thoughtful discussion, they understand that this problem is closely aligned to a Common Core standard: *constructing viable arguments and critiquing the reasoning of others.* This key practice becomes the focus of their Rounds group, and they use the following strategy:

Step 1

The team learns how to observe a lesson on video.

Step 2

The team focuses on their problem of practice, having reached the understanding that in general teachers do not consistently provide *daily differentiated rigorous tasks* that encourage students to explain their mathematical thinking and build math fluency.

Therefore, the team will begin by investigating the following question:

"How do we use Number Talks to plan for math discussions that enable students with different math abilities to explain their thinking and build fluency?"

Possible areas of focus for the observers:

- How does the teacher model the use of high-level math vocabulary so students can use it independently when they explain their thinking?
- How does the teacher listen to and follow students' math thinking?
- What procedures are in place to allow students to share their thinking?
- What conditions are present that foster a safe learning community?
- How is student communication encouraged and valued?

Step 3-A

The host teacher completes the Host Teacher Preparation Form.

Step 3-B

The host teacher videos her class doing Number Talks.

Step 4

The teachers convene a Rounds debrief meeting (See First Rounds Debriefing Protocol, Figure 5.4).

Observation

Teachers report what they've seen (without interpretation), with a particular focus on their agreed-upon problem of practice.

Wonderings

Here are just a few of the things teachers wondered about and how that thinking could impact their practice:

Host Teacher Preparation Form

1. Review/explain the problem of practice.

With the goal of building on number relationship to solve problems while building efficient strategies, we will investigate how we use Number Talks to plan for math discussions that enable students with different math abilities to explain their thinking and build fluency.

2. Provide context for the lesson.

- What is the task?

Using "mental math," students will solve the equation $368 + 191$. Students show a visual cue when they are ready with a solution, and students signal if they have found more than one way to solve the problem. This form allows students to think, while the process continues to challenge those that already have an answer. I collect answers correct/incorrect and record them. Students share their strategies and thinking with their peers.

- What is your role as the teacher?

My role is to act as a facilitator, questioner, recorder, and learner, in addition to creating a safe and accepting classroom community.

- What are the students going to be doing?

Students will reason with numbers and make mathematically convincing arguments. Students will be listening to their peers' responses and sharing mental math strategies.

3. On what should the observers focus their attention?

- How do I listen to and follow students' math thinking?
- How do I encourage and value student communication?
- What conditions are present that foster a safe learning community?

NOTE: On this Host Teacher Preparation Form, there is no Step 4—"To what extent should/would you like observers to interact with students?"—because this team is using a video.

- I wonder how you're going to make sure kids are using the most effective math tool, rather than the one they're most comfortable with.
- I wonder how you'll keep track of what happens during one Number Talk and how it affects the next one, based on what happens.

- I wonder how you can get students with a communication disability to express their thinking.
- I'm wondering how can you get students to commit to try new strategies—a different strategy?

Teachers Share Their Learnings

- I want to emulate four quadrants (way of recording on the whiteboard) so kids could see there were differences among strategies.
- There's a benefit to write what kids were saying while they were saying them. I learned it's important to connect those two things while they're doing them.
- I want to emulate some of the language she used about defending their answers and when a student realizes they made an error, there was no judgment or tone; it was just, "So you changed your mind," or using language of agreement.
- I want to emulate the clarifying questions she asked.
- I learned that the kids seemed to be fine with the routine—fine with the expectation that they were not being recognized for the quality of a response.
- I want to emulate the pace of the lesson. I think the video is only 7 ½ minutes long, and 20 out of 24 students answered. It felt brisk but never felt rushed. It felt like there was enough time.
- The assistant principal noted: I learned that this process of videotaping and wondering can be useful—a mentee can wonder about a mentor's practice in a collaborative fashion.

At the end of the round, each teacher makes a commitment to change his or her practice.

Commitments

- I commit to doing Number Talks with my own group and the lower group together. I'm going to attempt to do it with the whole group with fractions and see what happens. I want to facilitate so my students share air time.
- I'm going to try to do Number Talks with nonjudgmental words and tones—neither positive nor negative.
- I'm going to try to do Number Talks with less check-in with students to see how that affects the pacing.

- Instead of writing in quadrants and numbering the different strategies, I will ask students to name the strategy and record that. To build the skills of the four silent students, I'm going to video one student in an individual Number Talk and then re-video in a few weeks, and then record him in a group.
- I'm going to do Number Talks in small groups. I will see if it works well. I want to do it in small groups before I do it as a whole class. (Special education teacher)

Step 5

The next Rounds meeting begins with *records of practice* that teachers bring to report on their commitments.

Some Examples of Records of Practice

Two artifacts:

Video: She videoed a student who had trouble participating in Number Talks and how he was able to respond all on his own. She felt it could build up his confidence; he did better than she thought he would when he was by himself (on the video, her record of practice). She wondered about trying a few Number Talks with just a few of the kids that aren't as confident as the others.

Photo: From whiteboard, showing strategies named by students.

Video working on pacing and picture of solutions on whiteboard. The question she is working on is finding a balance between brisk pacing and ensuring a majority of students understand. She said she is particularly interested in this because she teaches students in the bottom third of math performance for the grade.

Host teacher's video reflected her commitment of combining two groups and a photograph of the whiteboard.

These teachers see that taking the time to work a handful of high-yield strategies into their routines will benefit their students tenfold.

Appendix F

Alex's Host Teacher Preparation Form

Rounds: Host Teacher Preparation Form

Name: Alexandra   **Date of Round:** October 2012

1. Review/explain problem of practice

I have two very different Advanced Algebra 2 classes. My I block class, which you will observe, has a set of students who possess a range of abilities and confidence levels for math (unlike my smaller J block class of the same course). I've had difficulty getting students to think for themselves and overcome challenges on their own. I see this trend when I ask them to practice what they have learned by applying content concepts to problems in the text, on worksheets, and so on. It seems to me that when students encounter something they don't understand, they call out for me rather than investigate the problem on their own, in partner, or with their "pod" (group of four). I would like them to increase their reliance on themselves and their peers for answers, explanations, and clarifications about the math rather than always turn to me.

2. Provide context for the lesson

We have just started our formal work on functions. Before Thanksgiving break, the students had two introductory lessons and a quiz on previous material. They will be coming back from the holiday without having completed any HW or preparation for the class. Additionally, the work we did before the holiday was not mastered by the students. We will be doing the following:

- Reviewing terms/definitions and notations related to functions
- Going over HW problems they did not successfully complete on their own a week before break
- Moving on to the concept presented in the next section by working on a framing activity
  - o Working in pairs/groups on the puzzle/real-world example
- Going over the puzzle, its answer, and what we can conclude

I will also provide explicit directions for the activity, which is a bit of a change. Usually, I have the students just "get to work" rather than walk them through what they have to do. I anticipate that they will have difficulty setting up the puzzle algebraically. As a result, I will suggest that they use a generic amount of money to model the problem rather than attack it algebraically.

3. On what should the observers focus their attention?

I would like the observers to take notes that will help me answer the following questions:

- In what ways do I support students in their individual learning of what's being presented?
  - o How do I frame the learning for the students?
  - o What instructions do I give at different times during the lesson?
  - o What tools do I suggest for overcoming challenges?
- How do students support their learning and understanding of material? What types of questions do students ask during lecture (e.g., clarification)?
  - o How much "wait time" for processing do they give themselves? What instructions do I give them for working with a partner or group? What are students doing when they are working with partners on the activity or "For You to Do" questions?

- o Is there evidence of students getting "stuck"? If so, what is this evidence?
- o How many questions are brought to me? How many stay within the partnership or group?
- What types of questions do students ask during lecture (e.g., clarification)?
  - o How do I respond when a student/group brings me a question? Do I . . .
    - – Give guidance for how to find an answer to the question?
    - – Ask a question that will lead them to an answer?
    - – Go to the board to address the class?
    - – Ask the students what they did to address the question themselves?
    - – Answer the question?
- What am I doing when students are working with partners/groups?

4. To what extent should/would you like observers to interact with students?

Teachers can ask anything they need of students for clarification, but those interactions should be minimal.

Appendix G
Alex's Student Slides

24 February 2013 - Lesson 3.6 Review and 3.7

Goals:

- graph complex numbers on the complex plain
- visualize operations on complex numbers as transformations on the complex plain

Warm-Up

Let one root of a quadratic function be $11 - 2i$.

- What is the other root?
- What is the quadratic function that has these solutions? (assume it is monic and that the coefficients are all integers)

Those who understood this sort of problem on the quiz, please help your classmates!

30 April 2013 - Chapter 5B - Getting Started

Exploring Lessons 5.6 and 5.7

Goals:

- Graph an exponential function and determine the equation of an exponential function given two points on the graph

- understand and apply the concept of strictly increasing and strictly decreasing in understanding an exponential function

Warm-up:

Compare and contrast all you know about the following terms:

- linear function

- polynomial function

- exponential function

Appendix H

Alex's Sample of E-Mail Responses From Students

Sample 1

Q1: In what ways, if any, do the daily warm-ups assist your learning/understanding of class material?

The warm ups really help me especially because it reminds me what we have just learned in the previous classes and it gets my brain "math ready," which is great before we get into more difficult material.

Q2: In what ways, if any, do the daily goals shown at the beginning of class contribute to your understanding of the material?

The daily goals for me don't add a whole lot, they let me know if i learn the expected amount during class, and if i do not then i can go at home and go over the material, it is just a marker for me to see if i am all caught up with the learning

Sample 2

Here are my responses to the two questions:
Question 1: Although homework assignments provide a metric for determining my comfort level with the material, the daily

warm-ups often help to a greater degree, as I haven't been thinking about the material for a number of hours, and the questions provide a sense of spontaneity. Since I have not seen the material for a long period of time, the warm-ups allow me to figure out just how much of the info I have processed, and how fluent I am with using it in different situations. Likewise, the suddenness of the questions push me to think on the spot (unlike homework, which gives me time to work through everything).

Question 2: Unlike the daily warm-ups, I do not feel that the daily goals contribute to my learning. Instead, I feel that they interfere with me discovering these "goals" naturally, and I am therefore left trying to achieve a goal, rather than attempting to work through individual problems and discover the principle of the goal independently.

Sample 3

Sorry I took so long to get back to you, but hopefully these are helpful!

Q1: In what ways, if any, do the daily warm-ups assist your learning/understanding of class material?

I really like the daily warm-ups because they help me see if I understand the material from the previous night as well as give an opportunity to discuss things I don't understand. Additionally, the warm-ups help me become more comfortable with the material if I wasn't so comfortable with the homework, or help me understand the topic better in general if I struggled with the homework. The daily warm-ups are also a good way to transition from the previous night's homework to the topic we are covering in class.

Q2: In what ways, if any, do the daily goals shown at the beginning of class contribute to your understanding of the material?

The goals help a little in class, but sometimes it is hard to look ahead to what we are going to learn if we are starting something new that I don't understand yet. However, where the goals really help me are when going back to study for quizzes or tests, because then I can see if I understand the goals of the unit, and they also introduce what is on each powerpoint if I am trying to find a certain unit or helpful notes to study.

Feel free to follow up if this isn't clear or you want more information.

Sample 4

Here are my answers to the short survey:

*Q1: In what ways, if any, do the daily warm-ups
assist your learning/understanding of class material?*

I really like the concept of the warm-ups because depending on the type of class that we are having, for example review or learning a whole new lesson, they help me see what I do and don't know as well as what I need to solidify and work on. Another reason why I find them helpful is because I often get a little confused if a concept or idea is just explained verbally, so having a physical math problem to do or a definition to write out really helps me understand exactly what it is that I am learning.

Overall, I think they are a really good way to start the class!

*Q2: In what ways, if any, do the daily goals shown at the beginning
of class contribute to your understanding of the material?*

The daily goals help me in a different way than the warm-ups do. Although I often forget to copy the goals down word for word, jotting down the key words and knowing what they are allow me to know what I should have walked away knowing from that class. Also, if I feel that I still don't really know how to accomplish one of the goals, I know what I have to go over at home.

Notes

Preface and Introduction

1. Troen, V., & Boles, K. C. (2003). *Who's teaching your children? Why the teacher crisis is worse than you think and what can be done about it.* New Haven, CT: Yale University Press.
2. Troen, V., & Boles, K. C. (2011). *The power of teacher teams: With cases, analyses, and strategies for success.* Thousand Oaks, CA: Corwin.
3. City, E. A., Elmore, R. F., Fiarman, S. H., & Teitel, L. (2009). *Instructional rounds in education: A network approach to improving teaching and learning.* Cambridge, MA: Harvard Education Press.
4. Teitel, L. (2013). *School-based instructional rounds: Improving teaching and learning across classrooms.* Cambridge, MA: Harvard Education Press.
5. Troen & Boles, *The power of teacher teams.*
6. Luzer, D. (2013, April 26). Why are we still a nation at risk? Probably because we haven't addressed the risk factors. *Washington Monthly.* Retrieved from http://www.washingtonmonthly.com/college_guide/blog/why_are_we_still_a_nation_at_r.php
7. City et al., *Instructional rounds in education.*
8. Lord, B. (1994). Teachers' professional development: Critical colleagueship and the role of professional communities. In N. Cobb (Ed.), *The future of education: Perspectives on national standards in education* (pp. 175–204). New York: College Entrance Examination Board.
9. Westheimer, J. (2008). Learning among colleagues: Teacher community and the shared enterprise of education. In M. Cochran-Smith, S. Feiman-Nemser, & J. McIntyre (Eds.), *Handbook of research on teacher education: Enduring questions in changing contexts* (3rd ed., pp. 756–784). Reston, VA: Association of Teacher Educators; Lanham, MD: Rowman.

Chapter 1

1. Del Prete, T. (1997). The "rounds" model of professional development. *From the Inside, 1*(1), 12–13. Worcester, MA: Clark University.

2. The concept of a Rounds group working on a common problem of practice was created by Elizabeth A. City, Richard F. Elmore, Sarah E. Fiarman, and Lee Teitel and introduced in their book *Instructional Rounds in Education* (Harvard Education Press, 2009).

Chapter 2

1. Ball, D. L., & Cohen, D. K. (1999). Developing practice, developing practitioners: Toward a practice-based theory of professional education. In G. Sykes & L. Darling-Hammond (Eds.), *Teaching as the learning profession: Handbook of policy and practice* (pp. 3–32). San Francisco: Jossey-Bass.
2. Associated Press. (1996, March 20). Cooperating to cut bypass deaths. *New York Times.* Retrieved from http://www.nytimes.com/1996/03/20/us/cooperating-to-cut-bypass-deaths.html
3. Hill, H. C. (2009). Fixing teacher professional development. *Phi Delta Kappan, 90*(7), 470–477. (Quote on p. 470)
4. Killion, J., & Hirsh, S. (2012). *Meet the promise of content standards: Investing in professional learning.* Oxford, OH: Learning Forward, p. 3.
5. *Standards for Professional Learning.* (2012). Learning Forward. Retrieved from http://learningforward.org/standards#.UgDq8VOGH_c
6. Mizell, H. (2008, July 12). *NSDC's definition of professional development: The second dimension.* Remarks presented at a meeting of the National Staff Development Council's state affiliate leaders, Orlando, FL, p. 5. Retrieved from http://learningforward.org/docs/pdf/mizell7_08affiliates.pdf?sfvrsn=0

Chapter 4

1. City, E. A., Elmore, R. F., Fiarman, S. E., & Teitel, L. (2009). *Instructional rounds in education: A network approach to improving teaching and learning.* Cambridge, MA: Harvard Education Press.
2. Ibid.

Chapter 7

1. Husock, H. (2000). *How to use a teaching case.* Cambridge, MA: Harvard University, Kennedy School of Government Case Program, p. 2. Retrieved from http://www.ksgcase.harvard.edu/uploadpdf/teaching_case.pdf

Appendix D

1. City, E. A., Elmore, R. F., Fiarman, S. H., & Teitel, L. (2009). *Instructional rounds in education: A network approach to improving teaching and learning.* Cambridge, MA: Harvard Education Press.
2. Adapted from Troen, V., & Boles, K. C. (2011). *The power of teacher teams: With cases, analyses, and strategies for success.* Thousand Oaks, CA: Corwin.

Index

Page references followed by (f) indicate a figure.

About the Authors

Considered authorities on the subjects of teacher education, teacher leadership, and professional development schools, Vivian Troen and Katherine C. Boles deliver workshops on Rounds groups, teacher teams and teacher leadership, speak at conferences and seminars, and regularly consult with schools and school districts in the United States and internationally. As classroom teachers they founded one of the nation's first professional development schools to link colleges and public schools in partnerships for the preservice education of teachers as well as the ongoing professional development of veteran teachers.

Collaborators for over 30 years, they are the authors of *Who's Teaching Your Children: Why the Teacher Crisis Is Worse Than You Think and What Can Be Done About It* (Yale University Press, 2003), *The Power of Teacher Teams: With Cases, Analyses, and Strategies for Success* (Corwin, 2012) as well as numerous articles and book chapters on teachers and teaching. Most recently they have joined national leaders of professional organizations of educators, state education agencies, and universities in the Teacher Leadership Exploratory Consortium, convened by Educational Testing Service to develop model national standards for teacher leadership.

Troen directs the Teacher Learning Project at the Jack, Joseph and Morton Mandel Center for Studies in Jewish Education at Brandeis University, supporting school leaders in developing systems for supervision and evaluation to promote ongoing teacher learning for both novice and veteran teachers. As a consultant, she works with school districts and school leaders building school-wide capacity for teacher teams and rounds groups and addressing a wide range of issues surrounding professional learning.

Boles is a senior lecturer on education and faculty director of the Learning and Teaching Master's Degree Program at the Harvard Graduate School of Education. Boles writes and teaches about school reform, teacher education, and new forms of teacher leadership. Her work advocates for increased teacher collaboration and thoughtfully-developed teacher teams that will enable teachers to tackle the most difficult issues of teaching and learning. She received her doctorate from Harvard, and her courses examine the latest research on school reform, teacher education, teacher teams, and new forms of teacher leadership.

Contributors

Jacob Pinnolis is the Director of Teaching and Learning at Gann Academy in Waltham, Massachusetts, overseeing the supervision, evaluation, and professional development of the faculty. He teaches literature and philosophy, facilitates a Department Chair Rounds group, has facilitated Faculty Rounds groups, and has been a mentor and mentor coach. He taught analytic philosophy at the University of Florida and at Virginia Commonwealth University. Jacob has an A.B. in Philosophy from Harvard University and an M.A.Ed. in Jewish Education from the Jewish Theological Seminary of America.

Aviva Scheur is the Coordinator of Professional Development at Gann Academy. Her role includes facilitating a Faculty Rounds group, training and coaching Rounds facilitators, coaching department chairs and mentors, strategic planning of professional development, teaching classes and providing curriculum oversight for an international school partnership. She has mentored student teachers from Brandeis and other graduate programs. Aviva holds a B.A. in Psychology from Boston University, an M.Ed. in Counseling and Education from Georgia State University and an M.A. in Near Eastern and Judaic Studies from Brandeis University.

CORWIN

A SAGE Company

The Corwin logo—a raven striding across an open book—represents the union of courage and learning. Corwin is committed to improving education for all learners by publishing books and other professional development resources for those serving the field of PreK–12 education. By providing practical, hands-on materials, Corwin continues to carry out the promise of its motto: **"Helping Educators Do Their Work Better."**

Advancing professional learning for student success

Learning Forward (formerly National Staff Development Council) is an international association of learning educators committed to one purpose in K–12 education: Every educator engages in effective professional learning every day so every student achieves.